New Kid
In Town

New Kid In Town

Written by
MONTE ENGELSON
2009-2016

New Kid In Town
Copyright © 2018 by Monte Engelson. All rights reserved.

No part of this publication may be reproduced, stored in a retrieval system or transmitted in any way by any means, electronic, mechanical, photocopy, recording or otherwise without the prior permission of the author except as provided by USA copyright law.

The opinions expressed by the author are not necessarily those of URLink Print and Media.

1603 Capitol Ave., Suite 310 Cheyenne, Wyoming USA 82001
1-888-980-6523 | admin@urlinkpublishing.com

URLink Print and Media is committed to excellence in the publishing industry.

Book design copyright © 2018 by URLink Print and Media. All rights reserved.

Published in the United States of America

ISBN 978-1-64367-168-0 (Paperback)
ISBN 978-1-64367-167-3 (Digital)

Non-Fiction
17.12.18

Contents

Preface: "New Kid In Town" 7
Chapter 1: Memories 15
Chapter 2: Fraser Lake School 56
Chapter 3: Fraser Lake North 67
Chapter 4: Pinchi Lake,
 Correspondence School 70
Chapter 5: Vanderhoof School 80
Chapter 6: Victoria, South Park
 Elementary School 100
Chapter 7: North Vancouver,
 Lonsdale Elementary 103
Chapter 8: Qualicum Bay,
 Dashwood Elementary 105
Chapter 9: North Burnaby,
 Alpha Junior High 109
Chapter 10: Prince Rupert Bo Me Hi 112
Chapter 11: Bella Coola Sir Alexander
 Mackenzie High 115

Chapter 12: Queen Charlotte Islands.
             Masset High 179
Chapter 13: UBC 1957 189
Chapter 14: The University Summers 197
Epilogue 235

Preface

"NEW KID IN TOWN"

My children and grandchildren always asked me questions. "What did you do when you were young?" "Where is your home town?" "What was it like living way back then?"

I would answer them with such funnies as: "When I was a child we had to walk 5 miles to school and it was up hill both ways". "We didn't have electricity or running water".

"Oh grandpa, you must be kidding me."

Maybe I should write up some of these stories. This task kept getting put off. My dad, Harold Engelson wanted to write his memoirs but left the task for too long. A stroke occurred. He could no longer write or type. I tried to encourage him to start but met with little success.

In Bella Coola there was a First Nations Elder, Clayton Mack who too had a stroke. This left him bed ridden for the last years of his life. He told stories to his doctor and nurses. These stories were recorded and placed in order. Two books were than produced of his ramblings. I suppose Clayton was the reason the following was put together.

I better start before it's too late.

As the thoughts were put to prose another purpose of putting all this down came to be. Composing thoughts of ones past makes one think more of what makes a person who he is. I have no regrets. If my life had to be done again not much would be changed.

During my time growing up my family moved a lot. Twelve schools were attended. Most of these meant starting all over again after each relocation. The title, "New Kid in Town", was rather easy as I was always the new kid in town.

For others reading these words who are older than me, like Anne Marie, some of my memories will be a bit off. One tends to remember some occurrences and forget others. Some items come before others. Memories are of the good times. Bad times for little people are usually not remembered. My time in Fraser Lake was always one of peace and content.

Thanks to "The Story Lady", Beth Stewart, who has been telling me to put my thoughts down for many years.

Beth helped me with my words. My composing skills were not so hot. She told me, "Don't let that worry you. Just keep on typing!"

2012

Since this book was finished some more story has surfaced. This now has been added.

HME 2016

This is for my children,

Rodger Montgomery

&

Cordelia Anna-June

My grandchildren,

Dallas James

&

Anna Lucia

Key for the Map

1. Masset
2. Prince Rupert
3. Terrace
4. Kitimat
5. Hazelton
6. Smithers
7. Pinchi Lake
8. Vanderhoof
9. Prince George
10. Rivers Inlet
11. Anahim
12. Ocean Falls
13. Bella Coola
14. Jasper
15. Qualicum
16. North Vancouver
17. Victoria
18. Vancouver
19. North Burnaby
20. Seattle
21. Bella Bella
22. Burns Lake
23. Fraser Lake

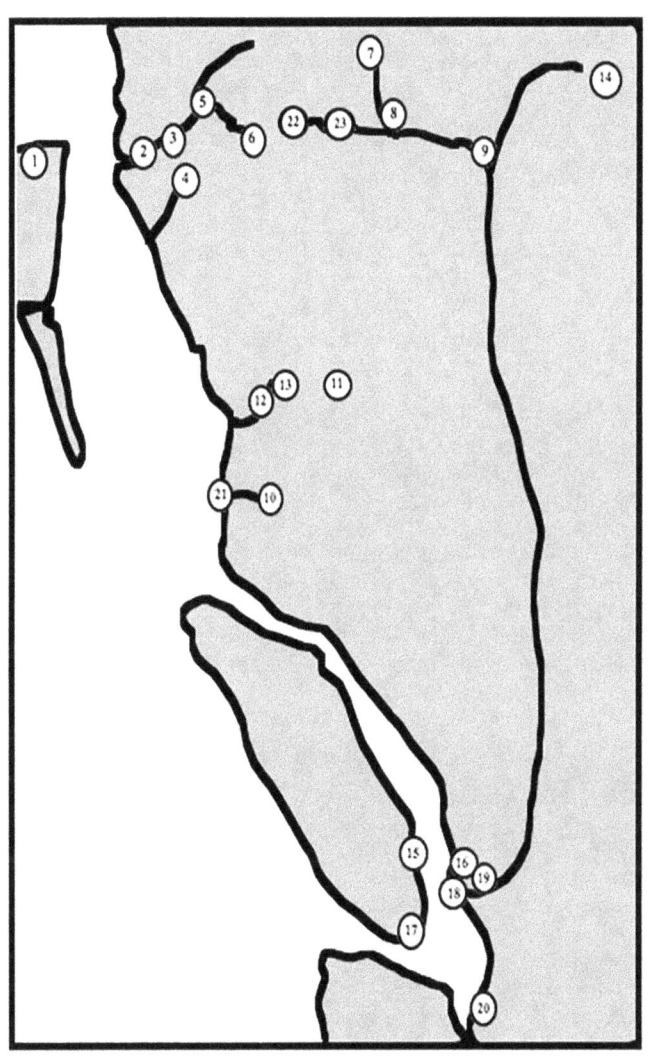

Map of most of the places in this book BC Southwest Quadrant

Chapter One

MEMORIES

Me, Harold Montgomery Engelson,
age, almost three

My first memories were just flashes and started in 1942. Mostly they were short bits which were different and made a big impression on my little mind: memories of this time are not all that clear. Some events listed below are not in order of time. These memories started when I was about three.

My mom trying to comfort me in a dust storm. I was scared. The wind was moaning and howling. The window was rattling. The lights went out. It was almost dark. Outside the window was just brown. Mom told me not to be scared. The wind won't hurt you. She slid up the rattling window and put her head out. The wind was roaring. The curtains were flying. Dust blew in the window. There was a large flash of orange light. In the brown outside power lines were jumping up and down. Mom screamed. The window shut. Bang! Mom hid under the bed covers with me.

Later, I asked questions about this time. The year had been 1941. We were in a hotel in Regina where Dad was learning how to fly so he could go to War.

Another memory was being awakened by Mom and Dad. I was sleeping in a drawer. They had been out. Dad gave me a large brown Teddy Bear.

This was on training leave. We were staying in a hotel in Edmonton or maybe it was visiting an aunt in Prince Albert.

Mom and Dad had gone out. Dad won the bear playing ring toss at a fair. I never did find out if I was "baby sat" or not.

When Dad was in training and on a leave a house was bought in Vancouver on Dunbar. Mom was to stay there for the War. The house was fairly new with an unfinished upstairs and basement. About this time I changed from a little boy to my mom's big man. I tried to act "grownup" but all I did was scowl a lot. Mom called me her " big man". A frown could be seen on my face on most all pictures of me taken until Dad got back from the War.

This pic was taken at house on Dunbar in Vancouver where the bit following occurred. This shows family that came up from Seattle to visit with their brother.

Playing in my mom and dad's trunk which was filled with lots of neat stuff. The trunk was up some stairs in a room with just boards for walls. The light came in through a window. The trunk was so big that I had to climb on a box to get in. Christmas decorations, toys, letters, movie film and just stuff. I had been told not to play there. So I guess that is why I did it. I made a big mess. I unwound the movies too. Mom came up the stairs and saw the mess. I ran down stairs, shut the door and turned the key in the lock. I went outside and ran away from the house. I came back. Getting cold and hungry. Mom was leaning on the window ledge of the upstairs room, telling me to go in and turn the key in the lock. I knew how to do that because that is how I got into the upstairs.

This I did and ran outside again. I came back in at dark. Mom was sitting on a kitchen chair and did not look too pleased with me. I don't remember much after that.

The unfinished upstairs was locked. A big skeleton key usually was on a nail hanging up so I couldn't reach it. This time the key had been left in the lock. I unlocked the door and climbed up the stairs. I was three years old.

A knock at the door. I went and opened it. My favorite uncle was on the porch on his knees to give me a hug. I climbed on his back and I rode him in. He was singing a song... "Horsey Horsey Crazy Over Horsey." He was in his navy captain's clothes.

Uncle Bob was a skipper on a RCN boat

Later that night my mom went down town with Uncle Bob. I was babysat by Wilma. When we stayed in Vancouver on Dunbar, two girls stayed with us Wilma and Iya. (ee-yuh).

For awhile we had a third. Her name was Dorothy Strom.

Uncle Bob and Mom went out and had a record made of the two of them singing. They sang "You Are My Sunshine" and a Swedish song. After, the record was sent to Dad who was in Regina. I still have the record some place but it was played too much and doesn't make much sound now.

I found it! The recording made by Mom and Uncle Bob

After the war Uncle Bob took Mom and I down to see his Department of Transport ship, the Estevan. He showed us everything. He took me all over and told the men on the boat I was his "nephew". We even went down to see the *engines. I was scared of the black men that were shoveling coal into the furnace.*

The Estevan

I later found out that the black men were really white but covered with coal dust. At this time coal was used to provide heat to run the steam engines. Uncle Bob was first mate on the Estevan after the war. This ship was the light house and marker buoy tender for the Canadian Pacific Coast.

Waking up to laughter. I climbed out of bed and peeked in the kitchen. Mom and Wilma and Iya were there with two men in air force uniforms. They were eating a large watermelon and spitting the seeds into the sink. I had never seen a watermelon. I was given a slice. One man gave me a set of airplane cards. The airplanes on the cards were black. He taught me their names.

The man that gave me the aircraft identification cards was married to Wilma. He came to our place when on leave from training. Wilma came from Fraser Lake, Mom's hometown. His name was Harold, same as my dad's.

Air Craft Identification Cards

The above cards are Japanese. There were card sets for USA, Germany, England, and Japan

We went to a beautiful building covered in lights. Inside there were red carpets and everything was gold. It was so pretty everyone talked real quiet. We had to wait in line a long time. I got some popcorn. Finally we climbed some wide tall stairs. A lady in a uniform with a big flashlight took us through some big doors and we sat in some soft seats. We were up really high. The stage was way down. The lights slowly went out. We were all quiet when a man came on the stage. He was wearing a tall hat. Nothing much happened for a long time so I fell asleep. Mom woke me up and said, "Look! Look!" There were elephants on the stage!

This was in the Orpheum Theatre in Vancouver. I was told later that we went to see Ringling Brother's Circus on stage.

Later Mom took me to see movies at the Orpheum like Lassie, and Bambi... I didn't like the Three Stooges. The Three Stooges weren't nice at all.

She was always taking me shopping. I was tired and cried. I wanted to go home. I fell down on the floor and screamed lots. Mom spanked my bum. An old lady ran over and hit Mom with an umbrella.

"Going shopping" was quite an event. Everyone got dressed up. Back in these times and living in the city a car was not used very much. Mom couldn't drive one anyway. There were three ways to travel, by foot, by streetcar or taxi. The streetcar ran right by our house. These were train

cars that ran on steel rails and received power from an electric wire that ran overhead. To get on a streetcar one had to wait on the sidewalk at a "streetcar stop". When the driver, called a "conductor" saw a prospective passenger he would stop and you would have to run out to the middle of the street to get on.

Waiting to board a streetcar

Mom took me to get a haircut... The man was wearing a white coat and sat me on a board on the big chair. He wrapped me up in a white sheet. He smelled bad. I didn't like him. He didn't like me either cause I screamed and pulled away and he pulled my hair real bad. I screamed more and threw up all over his white sheet. I didn't get my haircut.

Mom was scared and sometimes crying. Air Raid sirens made a scary moaning... a knock at the door. I ran to open it. I thought it would be Uncle Bob. It wasn't Uncle Bob. It was a strange man in a long black coat and an army helmet on his head. He scared me. I ran away.

The greatest fright of the war occurred on 20 June 1942, when a British vessel was torpedoed in the Strait of Juan de Fuca. On the same day, a Japanese submarine shelled the lighthouse at Point Estevan, a remote spot on the west coast of Vancouver Island. This was the only recorded instance during the Second World War of an attack from the sea on the West Coast of Canada. Vancouver was under a blackout. As everyone thought that the Japanese would soon attack, all windows had to be covered or lights left off. Our basement light was on and there were no blackout curtains there. The strange man was an ARP man (air raid precautionary) telling us to turn out our basement lights. Another reason my mom was worried was that money was supposed to come from the airforce and it didn't. Another was we had run out of wood for the furnace and sawdust for the kitchen stove. No heat. I remember how cold and damp it was. We finally got some wood. This was in big rounds and filled with knots. Grandpa and Uncle Bob, when they came to visit always ended up in the basement chopping wood.

Soon after this our house was put up for sale and Mom and I went to live north in Fraser Lake until after the war. We travelled up to Fraser Lake with a family friend, Billy Strom, He was just sixteen. He lived in Prince George. He had come to Vancouver by train to take a new truck up to his dad, Lars Strom, who was in the logging business.

Billy brought this new truck to our house. Billy tied our one suitcase to the spare tire on the truck frame. The truck was green. I sat in the middle. We were off. The truck made lots of truck noises and was very bouncy.

I woke up. It was dark. The truck motor was whining. I was looking at a dancing red light on the dash. I fell asleep. Daylight. The truck had stopped.

No Gas!

I got hungry and started to cry. I usually got my own way when I did that. Billy wasn't there. Mom and I got out and walked a long way along a dusty road. It was hot. Mom was wearing a grey suit, a black hat and high heels. We went to a big farm house. Mom knocked on a door and asked for some food for me. A nice lady gave me a glass of warm milk.

Billy, driving this new truck, took a wrong turn going through the Fraser Canyon. We got on the Blue Lake Road that went up to a mine. *By the time we got out and back on track we didn't have enough gas so the engine quit. Billy walked on ahead to find some fuel. Mom was wearing nice clothes because in those days one didn't travel without dressing up.*

We got to Fraser Lake and my Uncle Louie was in the town to take us to the farm. I really liked Uncle Louie. He was always teasing me but in a happy way. He called me a little squirt. He rowed us across the lake. I met my cousin Larry. A new kid! We glared at each other and didn't say a word. Everyone made a big fuss over me. "Oh look at the cute lil poika" That made me squirm and hide in my mom's dress.

"Poika" is Swedish for "little boy." Everyone up there spoke Swedish when in their own homes. I liked the farm much better than Vancouver.

Me at Fraser Lake, notice the frown.
More about this picture later

Another wakening. I was sleeping in a crib this time. Dad woke me up and gave me some things he called mitts. They were way too big and heavy. Dad said they were for playing baseball. What is baseball? There were also sets of boxing gloves. I had seen these used in the movies. He picked me up and gave me a hug and kiss. He was wearing his Air Force clothes. The wool coat was scratchy.

Mom and I are sad.
Larry just likes his picture taken.
Dad was now a navigator

Dad had finished his training and was going away to war. The crib and the strange gifts happened in Fraser Lake at my Uncle Louie Dahlgren's farm. Dad was catching the early morning train and was on his way to the

East Coast to go over to England on a big ship called the Queen Elizabeth. I was only three. What would I do with that stuff? Dad gave sports equipment to me because he thought that he might not be coming back. The baseball gloves were for a right handed person.

I turned out to be left handed...

Larry and I did have fun with the boxing gloves. Uncle Louie showed us what they were for. He tried to teach us how to box, you know, protect your face and do the jabs. Larry and I found out that "hay makers" worked better, and one properly delivered would knock the receiver flat.

Early morning- Dad catching train for Halifax. Uncle Bob, Dad, Aunty Ruth and Mom. Uncle Otto taking the picture. A sad time and trying to be cheerful at the same time. Chances are that dad wouldn't be coming back.

My memories were coming faster by this time.

Winter time and Christmas. I remember crawling behind the Christmas Tree. The floor was shiny and smelled of wax. My head bumped a glass ornament. It fell on the floor and broke.

Time with cousin Larry and his older sister Anne Marie. One night when her mother and father and my mom went to a dance, she babysat us. In the winter the kitchen was the only room in the house that was heated. Bedrooms were cold and only used for sleeping. Larry and I were sitting at the kitchen table having a bedtime snack of a bowl of krem (Swedish fruit soup. Really good) Anne Marie was talking to us and did a good job of scarin' the bejeezus out of us. She told us a ghost story. You have to remember at this time on a farm in the north there was no electricity. Our light at night came from coal oil lamps or white gas lanterns. These gas lamps had to be pumped up every once in awhile or the light got dimmer and dimmer. They made a hissing sound too. The light was fading when Anne Marie told us this story of huge wolves that would sneak into a house at night and eat little boys.

"What's that? I hear something." A rustle in the wall. "Something is coming!" Shhh..." Of course our little minds imagined the worst.

"I better go upstairs and see what it is." Anne Marie disappeared into the gloom and we could hear her slowly going up the stairs. Then... nothing...nothing for the longest time. A groan from up above... A thump.... the light was slowly fading away. Larry and I were hugging each other in panic. Something was coming down the stairs. We could hear it panting...We could see it in the stairway. Grey fur. " Oooooohhhh" Then a scream! Anne Marie had come down the stairs under a wolf skin... The two of us, Larry and I, went into absolute hysterics. We did not return to normal for a week.

The next time the family went to a dance Larry and I refused outright to be babysat by Anne Marie. We had to go along. The horses were hitched to the buckboard sleigh. There were Uncle Louie, Aunt Caroline, Ann Marie, Larry and I. We went to Grandpa Dahlgren's farm and took Grandpa and Granma too. Lots of snow was coming down soft and slow. We started across the frozen and snow covered lake.

I liked riding in the sleigh behind the horses. Larry and I were snuggled down in the hay to keep warm. You could smell the cold and the hay and the bear skin and of course the horses when they made horse buns. The horses were snorting and blowing steam in the air. Wind was blowing some of the hay away. It was dark. The grownups would talk in Swedish but most of the time they were quiet. Every so often Larry and I peeked out from the bear skin. The wind made a deep whistle sound as it blew across the snow. The wind got stronger and the snow was blowing sideways. The grownups sounded worried. Grandpa was holding a gas lantern up high to try and see through the falling snow. I pretty soon fell asleep.

The sleigh was loaded with hay and blankets. Larry and I were keeping warm under a bear skin. We had left in daylight but the light soon disappeared. Snow was falling thickly and getting deeper. The pretty snow turned into a raging blizzard. I can remember Grandpa standing up with a gas lantern trying to find the branches that were stuck in the snow to mark the trail. These disappeared. The horses kept turning to put their backsides to the wind. A trip which was to take an hour took all night. I don't think we got to the dance...I do remember being at other dances. In a back room of the dance hall was a big bed. Kids were put on this bed with the coats and went to sleep.

The winters were very cold. In Grandpa's and Uncle Louie's houses there was only a kitchen stove for heat.

Both places had a "parlor" a special room with nice stuff in it. This was only used for special occasions and had a "space heater." At night the fire in the kitchen stove would die down and had to be got going in the morning. There was no central heating at this time. Lots of blankets were on the beds. Us kids got mattresses stuffed with straw until we stopped peeing the bed... When it got real real cold we all slept together. In the morning we took our clothes to the kitchen. We slept in long underwear with pajamas over top and wore socks on our feet.

Spring was a time of melting snow and mud. Uncle Louie's International pickup truck was usually stuck or going to get stuck. Everyone wore rubber gumboots.

Soon though, warm winds came and dried up the mud. Grass grew and leaves came out and it was summer again.

On warm days with no wind the lake was like a mirror. Talking sounds could be heard from the other side of the lake. The farmhouse at Uncle Louie's was on a nice bay with lily pads growing in the shallow spots. Sometimes a beaver could be heard slapping his tail on the water. You never really saw the slap. Just a rainbow of spray on the water where the beaver dove. Uncle Louie told me they did this when diving to get away from danger. I think they did this when they were happy. In the still warm summer air fish jumped to catch bugs. There were lots of ducks and muskrats too.

In the real hot afternoons when the sky was summer blue, clouds would slowly grow puffing taller and taller. When they reached the sky the tops turned black and got big and flat. By evening maybe there would be thunder and lightning. That was always fun to watch.

Once in the summer while playing outside Grandpa's farm house I could hear a rumbling which got louder and louder and completely filled the air. At first I thought it was thunder. The noise was coming from the sky. I saw a plane and then another. The blue sky became filled with them all heading north. Planes with one engine. Planes with two and four. bombers and fighters. I watched them for a long time. Maybe dad was flying one of them. Mom and Grandpa and Grandma came out of the house to look.

The planes were flying to the air bases in Alaska to be closer to Japan.
I found out later that Grandma was not my real Grandma Dahlgren. The real Grandma died in Prince

George of a sick stomach, maybe appendicitis. This happened just after the move from Vancouver. My mom and her family came out to Canada from Sweden and then took the train to Vancouver. Mom went to school in Vancouver for a year.

After his house was built and some land cleared Grandpa put an ad for a wife in a Swedish newspaper. Soon he was in touch with a nice lady. She was a nurse in a hospital. She arrived in Fraser Lake and soon became my new Grandma.

Grandpa Dahlgren and Grandma
when they got married

In the mornings everyone listened to the 9 o'clock BBC broadcast on the battery radio to hear the latest war news. Everyone waited for Winston Churchill to speak. Everyone stopped talking, and looked worried when the news was on. I looked worried too.

Grandpa was nice to me. He spent lots of time in his shed. He had all his tools there. He made me toys out of wood. He made a boat with a paddle wheel, which I played with in the creek. In his shed there were some old wooden barrels. I climbed on a box and lifted a lid and looked in one. It was filled almost to the top with purple icky stuff that bubbled and burped and smelled like a batch of rising bread.

One day while playing in the yard two Indian ladies and two Indian men came to see us. Grandma and Mom invited the ladies into the kitchen. The Indians smelled different. Grandma and Mom gave them some old clothes.

Grandma put a piece of writing paper on the floor and I stood on it. She drew around my foot. This was given to the Indian ladies. They came back later with some nice moccasins for me. There were flowers on them made out of glass beads. The Indian men went into Grandpa's shed with some big cans of Saskatoon berries

The road around the lake went through an Indian village so I had seen Indians before. I found out later that the different smell was from wood smoke and the tanned skins they used to make moccasins and other clothes. The

icky stuff was Saskatoon wine that grandpa made for the Indians

Grandpa took me hunting grouse and squirrels. He made me pack the shot ones back. One grouse came alive on me. I was holding it by the feet. Grandpa told me to hit it against a tree...

Grandpa and Dad before the War

Grandpa and Grandma Dahlgren had a collie dog, Snooky, and a big black milk cow, Kusah. They had some chickens and pigs too. Every year Kusah had a calf. When the calf grew up and was taken away from her Kusah bawled, "Moowah! Moowah!" for a couple of days.

Grandpa and I would go for field walks too. He would go in the fall with a pitchfork and gather up loose hay for the cows. Once when finished the walk we stopped by his creek to look at fish in a deep quiet spot. He had made for me a fishing line with a string and a bent pin. He cut a willow stick for a fishing pole. A grasshopper was caught and placed on the hook. I put my line into the water.

Grandpa looked in the water and yelled, "Yeesus!" He stabbed in the water with his pitch fork and threw out a monster fish. Water was splashing all over and the fish was flopping on the bank. It wasn't a trout and it had a big mouth. It was bigger than me! A monster! I got scared and ran to the house.

This fish was a "burbot" better known locally as a "ling cod" because it looked like the cod that was caught on the coast. These were usually caught in the winter when ice fishing in the lake. These "cod" could grow to four feet long.

Sometimes we stayed at Grandpa's and sometimes at Uncle Louie's. Louie was mom's brother. I liked it better there because of my cousins Larry and Anne Marie.

We all got matching sleighs for Christmas one year. I wanted to sit on it to go. Uncle Louie showed us how to sleigh by lying down with our face forward. I told him that he was kidding us! I wanted to sit on it!

Me, Ann Marie and Larry on our new sleighs

Mom and I were walking back to Uncle Louie's from Grandpa's. We came across a porcupine waddling on the trail. We chased it almost all the way back home.

The farms were all homesteads. By the time I started school there were four of them. Grandpa Dahlgren was the first of the "Swedes". Then came Uncle Felix Johanson, Then came Uncle Louie Dahlgren's. Then came Uncle Jonas Johnson's. There was one in the middle belonging to Judge Peters. He was married to an Indian lady. He had lived there a long time and had lots of kids. Another homestead belonged to an Englishman, Mr. Ponsford.

Mr. Ponsford had a daughter, Bessie. She was very pretty. Sometimes I would walk over to their house. Bessie taught me how to play a game called "Snakes and Ladders"

Anne Marie looked after us, Larry and I. She made us wear her old dresses and made us drink stuff that she had squeezed from berries. That was terrible stuff.

Anne Marie and her brother Larry

Another time in our upstairs bedroom she got out a sleeping bag and enticed us to sleep in that with her. We were four years old. She was 12. She told us to go down to the bottom of the sleeping bag. She climbed in the top and let out some "gas".... We didn't trust her much after that.

Larry and I slept upstairs. We could hear the loons crying and the night freight train. When the lake was calm the train could be heard a half an hour before it passed the town. The train tracks were across the lake on the town side.

In our upstairs there was only one big room. There was an old wall clock that tocked all night. Every hour it would call out the time, "bung...bung...bung..." The clock went "tock-tick, tock-tick...."

Taken at the Lake, Uncle Louie's farm

In the winter time we would stay awake and listen to the clock and the train and the mice in the walls...If lots of snow, everything was real real quiet. We could tell when it got cold because the lake would make weird noises when the ice expanded. Cracks would zip across the lake making the most neat sounds. The house would creak and sometimes bang. Outside at night some trees would split with a loud crack that sounded just like a big gun going off. Some winters the lake would freeze with no snow, just smooth ice. We called it glare ice. The lake was

10 miles long so skating was great. You could shoot a hockey puck out of sight if the wind caught it.

Mom and Aunty Caroline were always horsing around. Larry looks a bit worried.

We, meaning us kids, didn't get up in the morning until the kitchen stove was crackling. We got dressed in the kitchen where the heat was.

Uncle Louie wasn't home much in the wintertime. He lived at a tie camp with his work crew.

Ties were the cross ties put under the railroad tracks. All the Swedes cut ties in the wintertime to make enough money to make it through till spring. Grandpa cut ties on his mountain behind the farm. In the springtime he put them on a sleigh and with the horses, took them to the railroad on the other side of the lake.

Aunt Caroline and Mom would go out and do the chores. On the farm there were lots of chickens. Aunty sold the eggs. We helped clean the eggs while Mom and Aunty "candled" them to check for blood spots...

The large chicken house had to be cleaned every day. Cows had to be milked and fed. Uncle Louie looked after the horses. These horses, two big work ones, did all the jobs on the farm as there wasn't a tractor yet. Uncle Louie or Uncle Joe would put Larry and me on the horses backs when our moms weren't looking.

NEW KID IN TOWN

Taken in Jasper, Me, Aunty Caroline and Larry

About this time Mom had to go down to Vancouver to sign some papers because the house on Dunbar was sold. So Mom and I and Aunty Caroline and Larry went down to Vancouver. We took the train from Fraser Lake to Jasper and from Jasper to Vancouver. We all had to dress up.

Travelling on the train was exciting. Larry and I could walk along the train cars. This was fun because the train was always rocking back and forth. It was noisy to go from one car to another. Big people had to help us. Our favorite train car was the one at the back of the train. It was called a "smoker car" and was like a big long living room. At the end was a door that went out to the back of the train. There was a metal fence so you couldn't fall off. The train made a different noise here. The wheels sang "clickclick–clickclick–clickclick."

Another car was neat. This was the dining car. There were tablecloths on all the tables and a nice man was our waiter. He taught Larry and I our "table manners".

Our car was a "Pullman" car. This was changed to a bedroom each night. Mom and I got the top bed and Aunty Caroline and Larry got the bottom. Larry and I really liked the "porter". He was the man that made the Pullman car into a Sleeper. This man was a big black man. We stared at him a lot. Our moms told us it was impolite to stare. The only place I had seen a black man before was in the movies. Larry had never been to a movie so I had to explain all about black people. On the way back to Fraser Lake we took a Canadian Pacific boat to Prince Rupert. We were in a cabin aboard. The weather was bad. There was lots of wind and rain.

The sea was rough and the boat went up and down and tipped this way and that. A "steward" not a "porter" made the beds up at night and put them away in the morning. I didn't like this trip at all. I was sick the whole way. Every time I got out of bed I could feel the boat move and I threw up. After awhile there was nothing left to throw up but I did anyway. At the end of the boat ride we took the train from Rupert to Fraser Lake.

Sometimes we would go to the other side of the lake. In the summer we would row across the lake or go around it in Uncle Louie's pickup truck. In the wintertime we would walk across the lake. This was fun but cold. Mom and Aunty Caroline put so much clothes on Larry and me that we could hardly walk. Aunty Bert was living and cooking in the cookhouse for the town's large sawmill. We stopped there for lunch. We went to the general store. In the middle was a big stove. Around it would be Indians who came in to get warm and look at stuff.

Fraser Lake Store. Uncle Louie's truck in front

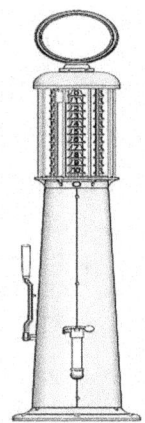

In front of the store there was a gas pump. The top half was glass. There was a big lever on the pump. A man would move the lever back and forth and gas would be pumped into the glass top. This had numbers down one side. If you wanted five gallons, this amount was pumped into the top.

Mom made me a sailor suit. I was real proud of the suit but didn't like everyone saying, "Ohhh, isn't he cute".

The next photograph was taken when Mom and I went down to Seattle. We were always going someplace This picture was taken at Uncle Viv's and Aunty Thelma's farm at Concrete, Washington. During this time our family traveled frequently to the States where Grandma Engelson and Dad's brothers and sisters lived. I know this from photographs. I will see if can find some of those pictures. This would be a good place for them, as I am soon to start school. Little did I know that I would go to 12 different ones

Me and Uncle Vernon
I was four, maybe five

I always liked returning to the north country after a trip to the coast. I wasn't the new kid in town here. The air was cleaner. The sky was blue instead of grey. The clouds were big and fluffy. One could lie down in a hay field and look at all the animals in the clouds. Most times we went around with bare feet and when walking could feel the dust with our toes. Sounds were cleaner. Thunder's so loud you could feel it in your bones. Grasshoppers could be heard flying, "crack crack crack crack crack". Houses were filled with the smell of bread baking. No one missed electric lights. I did miss indoor plumbing… Larry laughed at me when I told him about an indoor toilet. He didn't see one until we all went down to Vancouver.

Mom and Dad, Aunt Marguerite and Uncle Bob, Uncle Jack and his wife, Aunty Caroline and Uncle Louie, 1945

Dad and Uncle Louie, me, Mom and Aunty Caroline and a "CooCoo" Comic

I remember my fourth birthday. Grandma made me a cake with lots of icing. I got a cowboy suit and some guns. Afterwards I told everyone I was three again.

Chapter Two

FRASER LAKE SCHOOL

Next year, Mom and I moved from the farm to town across the lake. Mom worked in the Fraser Lake General Store. I was put into the one room schoolhouse and taught (babysat) by the students and the teacher, Mrs. Black. There was no kindergarten back then. More letters came. Some were from Dad. Others were from my favorite Seattle grandma. She always mailed me stuff. I put together a collection of these letters. I call it "Letters from Mother". It can be found on the internet at www.engelson.ca.

This is the primary gang at the school. Most of the sixes had lost their front teeth by this time. I still had mine.
I am front right with the two-tone hat.

For Christmas when I was five I got a pair of skis. One weekend we had races. The race I was in was on the road in town. It started at the water tower and ended in front of the store. I think I came in last, but it was fun...

MONTE ENGELSON

The great skiers! Larry and I
This was taken when we were six

On the next page is a letter that mom sent to dad. I told her what to put down.

Feb 3, 1945

Dearest loving Daddy,

I am so glad to hear you are coming home so when you get home I will throw my arms and legs all over you what do you think of that!

I know how to cook poached eggs so when you get home that's all you will get from me.

I love you so much daddy I will just kiss you when you come home. I have got a cold.

At the ski race I won a yellow ribbon and ten cents. Mama won a purple ribbon and two dollars. I wish you could have come with us to Mrs Pratts because she had ice cream. I will be good to Mama and AnneMarie

With a bundle of love from your son Monte

Finally we heard that Dad had done his "tour". He was on his way home. The War was not over but the end was in sight.

Here is the last letter that mom wrote to Dad:

March 29, 1945

Hello my darling,

   I got one letter saying you didn't know and one you did. That you were practically on the way home. Then the next mail I got the pictures addressed to you. So I of course tore them open right then and there and darling you look rather pale and tired and thin, but you also look just as loving as ever and when I look at you I practically lose my breath. Every one in town has been to see your pictures at the store I just showed them to everyone and I'm so doggone proud. Monte he looked and said "Daddy" in the most hold your breath way. Gee is it windy. The paper is just practically dancing off the table. The roads are awful. The lake is impassable and huge sides of dirty snow line the road. The middle is just mud. But all the same tomorrow is Good Friday and I don't work. As soon as I get a wire I'll just walk home and start house cleaning so I won't have to do any the first day you are home. I'll also try to do some baking. The staff at the store are planning a party for you. I think to get you plastered. I wish you and I could get them laying in the aisles instead. I bet you could with you pouring and me making them down the hatch. Remember! Gosh! Are we going to have fun or are we! Well anyhow, Dad put on a batch of beer as soon as he knew you were coming for sure.

All my love, Anna

Here is Dad's last letter. This was written from Montreal to his mother in Seattle.

Montreal April 1st 1945

Dear Mom

Am on my way home at last. Arrived back in Canada on the Queen Elizabeth, Leaving on tonight's train. Had a good if rough trip over and have just now finished having 3 milkshakes, 2 banana splits and 1 steak in the last hour. Pretty good huh...

Will most likely be in Fraser Lake a couple weeks before we go south unless Anna wants to go right away. I have until the 16th of May on Leave and am pretty sure I can get my discharge soon after.

Train is soon due to leave so hello to you all

Love Harold

The Queen Elizabeth was the largest passenger ship in the world. It was changed into a troop transport ship during the war.

April 1945, Dad sent a letter from Montreal from a train station. Soon after Dad was home. He beat his letter back to Fraser Lake. He did "wire" ahead to tell when he was arriving.

I have to remember who I am writing this for. "Wire"? This was a form of telephone communication somewhat like text messaging. At this time there was only one telephone in Fraser Lake. The railroad had stations which could "text message" These messages were printed and then given to those who they were for.

Dad got off the train wearing his officer's uniform and packing a duffel bag. I thought that he would pay me some attention but most of his time was spent kissing mom. I got a bit jealous with that. He brought back some pictures too. Dad did the best to explain them to me. Here are some of them.

Dad's Beaufighter or one like it

Dad had a dog that a lady in Scotland had given him. Dad named the dog Beau. The dog was always waiting for them to come back after a mission. One day when starting the motors the dog kept jumping up and barking at one engine. The dog was killed by the propeller. Both Don and Dad refused to fly in that plane. Another crew flew that plane and were never seen again.

Don Acker, Dad's Pilot and Dad

Dad sat in the bubble half way back.

A Battle Picture

Dad on top right. This picture was in lots of newspapers

Later I got to sit on his knee for quite some time while he emptied his duffel bag. Some presents were for Mom, and for me, a pilot's helmet. This was a leather thing. I was hoping for a metal army helmet. It was a present from another pilot who gave him the helmet to give to my dad's little boy, Monte. That pilot went up in the air and never came back...

Here it is.
Brother Brian used this for his motorcycle helmet.

Chapter Three

FRASER LAKE NORTH

For a while I was placed in a one room school house on the North Side of Fraser Lake. This is where all the homesteads were. The time in this school was not long at all. This was a typical one room affair. The teacher's name was Mr. Rhymal, I think. The class consisted of Larry Dahlgren and I and a whole bunch of Johnsons. Half of them were our cousins. The rest were a large family who were renting the Peter's place. Buster, Charlie, Sonny and Leroy. I think all the girls were named after flowers.

  Only one item of note happened here. One day Joanne and I walked to the school to play on the swing and the teeter totter. This was about a half mile. Getting close to dark we thought we had better get home. We just got out on the road and something was walking towards us. It was the biggest bear we had ever seen. We ran back inside the school. No one ever locked a door back then.

We waited and waited and waited. Every once in a while we peeked out the door. No bear. Oops, now it is too dark to go home. Cousin Ann Marie finally came looking for us and found us in the dark schoolhouse. She just took us home and told us that the bear was just something we had dreamed up.

Our formal portrait taken at Uncle
Joe's Homestead Me, Joanne & Lynne,
Larry, AnneMarie and little Allan.
Uncle Louie called us the Swedish Meat Balls.

The previous photo was taken after one of my family's trips to the coast. I was dressed up as usual. I was even wearing a "necktie". Staying over night this city kid complained because he did not have any pajamas. Aunty Bert got out one of Joanne's "nighties" and I had to wear it! How embarrassing! I didn't dare complain about anything again when Aunty Bert was around. She had a way to fix me good. She was real nice though.

Chapter Four

PINCHI LAKE, CORRESPONDENCE SCHOOL

Soon after coming back from the War, Dad joined with Uncle Louie and two other men, Mr. Vinnedge and Mr. Lepoidevin and bought Fraser Lake Sawmills. Because lumber was much in demand after the war lots of money could be made. We moved north to a small abandoned town called Pinchi Lake; Uncle Louie and family moved to Pinchi Lake with us too.

    This is where I started grade one. I did the whole thing through correspondence courses. The school was the kitchen table. Mom was my teacher. Larry didn't take the correspondence courses. Since Larry wasn't going to school, I read the Star Weekly comics to him on the weekends. At least Larry thought that I was reading.

When we arrived in Pinchi Lake Dad let Mom pick a house to live in. There were 150 empty ones. She chose a big log cabin close to the lake. The house was nice in the summer. In fact I thought the log "chinking" great. This chinking was moss. I pulled out a line of it so I could see out as my sleeping area didn't have a window. When winter came and the temperature got to sixty below the house could not be kept warm even after I put the moss chinking back in.

We also had some pack rats in the house. One night Dad shot one with a moose gun in the living room. Next year we moved into another house that was right next door to Uncle Louie's. This was not a log cabin.

Life in Pinchi Lake was fun. There was lots of trouble to get into. At least we found it. I can't believe that our parents turned us loose as much as they did. Pinchi was a closed down mine and smelter. There were lots and lots of empty houses. All the streets in town were covered with pink crushed rock.

In the spring of 1946 Grandpa Dahlgren died. We went back to Fraser Lake. I went too but didn't go to the funeral . After the church service the coffin was placed on the back of Uncle Louie's pickup and taken to the cemetery. I watched everyone go to the cemetery from a window of the house where we were staying. Everyone who was at the church, walked behind the truck. A big surprise for the townspeople was that the Indians who had waited outside the church all walked to the cemetery too. I guess that was because of Grandpa helping the Indians.

In Pinchi in the summer we went on fishing trips. The mill had a boat to pull booms of logs around. The boat was called Beneeja, at least that was how it sounded. I couldn't read yet. This was our fishing boat. Fishing was good in the lake with rainbow and kokanee trout.

One small stream was shown to us by the Indians. It was the home of kokanee salmon in the fall. These small fish went there to spawn. At one place by a waterfall anyone could catch them. Whites like us weren't supposed to but we did anyway. A great big washtub was filled with these fish. Everyone helped clean them. Larry and I cut their bellies open with scissors. They were canned in quart sealer jars.

There was an interesting old man, Mr. Brunlin, who lived in a real fancy house on the lake. He was the retired mine manager. He flew an old airplane that had an open cockpit and floats. All the planes up here had to land on water. Dad went with him on flights. I wasn't allowed. Dad said that the plane was too old. Sometimes Larry and I went to Mr Brunlin's house. He gave us cookies. His house was filled with stuffed animal heads. In front of a large fireplace was a tiger skin with a big head. Larry and I used to sit on the head and Mr. Brunlin told us stories of hunting in Africa. Afterward I would go home and look up the pictures from Africa in our encyclopedia set.

Pinchi Lake Mine and Smelter was on the side of a mountain. We weren't supposed to go near the buildings but we couldn't help ourselves. We went anyway. One day when exploring, Larry found a funny bit of gravel ground right next to the mine building. When we jumped up and down the ground jumped up and down too. We moved some of the gravel away with our hands and found that the rocks were "floating" on some silvery stuff. What is it?

We tried picking it up but the stuff slipped through our fingers. On the next day we returned with a spoon and a cup (my special baby spoon and a silver mug). I'm not making this up. I really did! With the spoon we managed to fill the cup. The stuff was too heavy to pack home. Later we came back with our wagon. A beer bottle was found and we spooned the silver stuff into it. Then we pulled the wagon home and showed the silver water to our moms. They recognized the liquid as the same stuff that was in a thermometer. It was called mercury. That was what was mined at Pinchi. They found the spoon and cup that we had used. We were now in more trouble. The silver spoon and cup weren't shiny any more. The cup Larry and I took with us was my silver baby mug. That was in worse shape than the spoon. The silver coating was gone. I had taken that metal cup because I knew that a glass cup might break. Our dads kept the bottle of Mercury for a long time.

This happened before the common knowledge was out that mercury was very poisonous. The cup and spoon were in sad shape because the mercury dissolved the silver right off the surfaces of the cup and spoon. The pink crushed rock on the street was cinnabar, mercury ore. A causeway out into the lake was made of this pink gravel. In fact all the tailings from the mine that weren't used for gravel were dumped in the lake. Tailings are what is left over after the mercury is smelted from the cinnabar. A short time after this everyone had to leave the area. The lake was closed to fishing and the local Indian village was moved to nearby Stuart Lake. We ate a lot of fish from the lake before we moved. I don't think that the mercury damaged us.

My grandpa Engelson came to live with us. He was a Klondike miner so liked living there. Larry and I would go on long walks with him and he would tell us about mining. In the abandoned town there was a bowling alley and a pool hall. Grandpa would take us there when he wanted to play. We didn't care for the pool hall as we were too short to see what was on the table. We liked bowling but all Grandpa taught us was how to set pins. The balls were too big for us to lift. I liked the noise of the balls hitting the pins.

One day Grandpa took me to the top of the mine mountain. We sat beside the "Glory Hole", which was the top of the open mine. It was a warm day. Mosquito hawks were feeding and diving, "Zeep" they went. I asked Grandpa if he got rich in the Klondike. He smiled and told me he made a million dollars. He sat in the warm sun with his arm around my shoulders

Grandpa Engelson on top of the mine mountain
Part of the town is along the lake

One August evening dad had to go down to the sawmill and start an old pump engine to water down the mill site. Someone had to do this each hot dry day so the mill wouldn't burn up. He cranked the old engine. The engine "back-fired" and threw the crank handle at him. This hit him below the eye and rebroke a cheekbone that had been shattered while crash landing during the war. He had to go to the hospital in Vanderhoof. The doctor there fixed him up pretty good. In fact he straightened out some bones from the accident in WWII.

The lumber cut in the Pinchi Lake sawmill all had to be trucked to Vanderhoof to be planed and finished. One day a truck was very late arriving at Vanderhoof. The driver said that a moose was blocking the road and wouldn't let the truck get by. Everyone laughed at this excuse. The next day another truck was stopped by the same moose. The driver honked his horn which was a bad mistake. The moose charged the truck. Wham! He broke a headlight. Then it broke the front window with its hooves. Now everyone believed the truck drivers.

Mom got pregnant when we were there. Brother Brian was born in the Vanderhoof hospital. She spent time in the hospital waiting for the baby to come too . Dad and I would drive down to Vanderhoof over the winter road. The snow banks on the side of the road were high. We saw lots of moose. They sure were ugly. They looked like they had been put together all wrong. Once we saw a huge gray wolf. It stepped over the big snow banks just like a moose would.

Brother Donald Brian arrived on May 24. He was named after Don Acker, Dad's pilot in World War II. When Dad brought Mom and Brian home from the hospital he bought for me a black Labrador dog so I wouldn't get too jealous over the new baby. The dog's name was Beau. He was named after my dad's plane when he was in the war. This plane was a Beaufighter. I still got jealous over Brian because he was born on May 24th. That meant he would have a holiday on his birthday every year.

This was Queen Victoria's birthday and always was a holiday. Not like now. May 24th is now celebrated on a Monday.

That first summer was the one for exploring and getting bit by mosquitoes. Both Larry and I got bit so many many times that sore bumps came up on our necks and under our arms.

One day we were throwing rocks. Larry threw one over a house. I tried to do the same and took out a window. Aunty Caroline saw us. We were playing inside one of the houses with another boy in town, Bobby Faith. His parents owned the store. They sold stuff to us and the Indians. Bobby was hiding on us. We were throwing stuff at him. I threw an old Prem can where Bobby was hiding. He popped up. The can hit him and almost took off his eyebrow. Larry and I ran home and left Bobby bleeding. More trouble.

I met Bobby a couple of years ago. He still remembers me and has the scar to prove it.

That winter a local big boy taught us how to snare small animals like squirrels. This boy was Tommy Carlson. We set our snares with Tommy on the railway. This railway went from the mill to the forest. Indians were paid to cut firewood for the smelter. Tommy would pay us for the squirrels we caught and we watched him skin them.

A snare is made from fine brass wire. It is a small lasso and could be tied to a small bush or branch. The small animals made trails in the snow. A snare could be placed in position on a trail and hidden. The rabbit, or squirrel would walk through the loop of wire. The wire would tighten and the animal could not get away. They usually froze to death.

One day Larry and I were following a game trail in the snow to Tommy's house. We set a snare on this trail. The next day we had caught one of Carlson's pigs. It was frozen and dead. Trouble always had a way of finding us.

NEW KID IN TOWN

The picture above was taken on Aug 31,
my seventh birthday.

Soon we had to leave Pinchi, maybe because of the mercury. Larry's family moved to Ft. St. James and our family moved to Vanderhoof. Dad was to manage a Planer Mill and Uncle Louie was to manage all the sawmills which cut rough lumber that went to the planer to be smoothed.

Chapter Five

VANDERHOOF SCHOOL

Well here it is September and I'm in Vanderhoof. Again I won't tell you all, just what made an impression on me.

I remember going to my first real school. No one took me to school as that would be embarrassing. There was no registration. You just had to show up. After talking to the principal, Mr. Thistlethwaite (students called him Whistlebait), I was sent to Miss Hardy's grade one classroom. In this classroom, seating was arranged by order of "smarts". That is best row, second best, third best, etc.

Because of my age and the fact that I already had taken schooling from Mom I was placed in the second seat of the best row. Margaret Teichrobe sat in the first seat. She came from a large Mennonite family. I think there were 20 kids in it. She was seven too, but didn't go to school the first year because they had forgotten to send her. At least that is what was told to me. I met her at a school reunion a couple of years ago. Two weeks later Margaret was moved to the grade two classroom. A month after that I was sent to the same class. The teacher's name was Mrs. Wilkes. She made you sit still.

Our house was on the outskirts of town, a log cabin. There was no power, but we did have running water of sorts. Right beside the sink in the kitchen was a hand operated pump. When we pumped the handle, water ran out. The well water was not good. The stuff tasted awful. We had an outhouse in the wood shed. This was a bit unusual because most outhouses were out in the yard. This was considered a luxury.

This was our log house in Vanderhoof.
Mom liked log houses.

I had to tie Beau up so he wouldn't go to school with me. Winter was fun. A next-door neighbour kid, Terry, had a big dog, Sport, that pulled a cart. It used to be the milkman's cart. The dog pulled the cart with Terry and I on it. This was much more fun than walking. Terry's dad was the "section foreman" for the railroad. Terry and I spent lots of time with the trains. These huge steam engines should be mentioned because they are not around anymore.

Terry, Sport, Grandpa Engelson, little Brian and I

Most stuff and people traveled by rail. The roads were just too poor. One trick the engineers would do to Terry and I was to let out a blast of steam close to scare us. Even if we went to Fraser

Lake we sometimes went by train. Going to Prince George was always by train. In Vanderhoof the ticket was bought at the train station. This was also the telegraph office where you could send Telegrams or "wires".

Lots of our weekends were spent at Fraser Lake. We liked it. My mom's sister, Brita, had three kids, so we stayed there as well as with Uncle Louie. Both these farms were on the lake. Aunty Bert, as we called Brita, was married to Uncle Joe, Jonas Johnson.

We liked this house best because it had a nice beach for swimming in front of it. Us kids spent a lot of our time playing in the water.

One of our favorite times was watching the thunderstorms. Joanne, Lynne, Allan and I would sit on the beach with a blanket over us and watch the far side of the lake and count the seconds between the lightning and the thunder. If we were lucky the sky would send down hail instead of rain. When that happened Aunty Bert would get all excited and have us all outside afterwards and collect the hail. This was put into the ice cream maker with fresh cream and soon we would have ice cream. Remember, we didn't have a refrigerator.

At least once a week she baked a cake. Us kids had to choose the color of the icing. She made tubes out of writing paper and filled them with icing so we could write on the cake. Our favorite colours for cake were red and blue.

Uncle Joe was building a large house for his family. He had a homestead close to Uncle Louie. The first year he built a two-room house for the five of them. And when company arrived like me and mom we all squeezed in. Sometimes the barn was used for sleeping.

A few years later he decided to build a bigger house. The place he picked for the house was solid rock. Uncle Joe spent his time making holes for dynamite. He used a special iron bar that he hammered into the rock to make the holes.

Each hole took him a day to make. We were staying at Aunty Bert's when Uncle Joe blasted for the first time. We didn't know what was going to happen. His new house was going to be 50 feet from the old house. Uncle Joe lit the fuse on the dynamite.

In the house Aunty Bert had us 4 kids and herself hide under the kitchen table. We waited and waited… nothing… The dynamite was no good. Back to Vanderhoof I went.

Later that year we came back to visit. Aunty Bert got all excited and was talking a mile a minute. We were all in the house, Aunty Bert, my mom and dad, baby Brian, Joanne, Lynne, Allan and I. Uncle Joe was outside tending to his dynamite. He lit the fuse without telling anyone in the house. "BOOM!" The house jumped sideways! Rocks hit the side of the house. We all screamed. The air filled with dust. Aunty Bert just kept talking as if nothing had happened. She talked a lot.

After about a year or so he stopped building on the house. The cellar wasn't used much after all that work. The kitchen and pantry were big and used all the time. There was the bedroom on the main floor for Uncle Joe and Aunty Bert. Upstairs was where us kids would stay. There was a fancy parlor that was only used at Christmas time. Again there was just the kitchen stove for heat. Uncle Joe blasted and drilled a well for water. The water tasted terrible like most well water. Lake water tasted just great. But you had to pack the lake water to the house in buckets.

Uncle Joe spent all his time working on the farm, except on Sundays. The only extra dollars came from his skill as a carpenter. He had polio when young and one leg was shorter than the other so he walked with a lurch and couldn't work in the sawmills. He also only shaved his whiskers once or twice a month.

Once Aunty Bert got sick and had to go the hospital. This left Uncle Joe to look after us kids. We didn't like his cooking because he liked fish head chowder the best. He would want us young uns to eat the eye-balls.

About noon on a Sunday he was looking out at the lake and saw a flock of ducks swimming close to shore.

"Vall" he says," I tink ve villl half some duck for dinner"

He got out an old shotgun, put some shells in it, walked down to the beach. Shot, "BAM! BAM!" He leaned his gun against a stump, took off all his clothes, except for his long johns, (underwear), and waded out in the water up to his chest to retrieve the four ducks that he had killed with his two shots. Still soaking wet he took the ducks to the house. Us kids, Joanne, Lynn and Allan and I looked at Uncle Joe with amazement. First shooting the ducks, then retrieving them the way he did. This was the only time we ever saw him go "swimming". We were pretty sure after that he never ever took off his long johns.

"Aren't you going to pluck them?" I asked.

"Naw, tew much verk." He then used a knife and skinned the ducks.

He took the ducks into the house, boiled up some new potatoes, cut up the ducks, placed them in a roasting pan and put it in the oven. Later he made some gravy Turns out that Uncle Joe was a great cook.

The only thing wrong with the meal was the buckshot left in the ducks. This meal was lots better than fishhead soup.

Here is another story about Uncle Joe. The time was winter. We woke up early in the morning in the dark. Aunty Bert was making a fire in the kitchen stove. Uncle Joe and Aunty went out to do the chores. This meant getting the eggs from their big chicken house, milking the cows and feeding all the farm animals. After awhile us four grabbed our clothes, ran down stairs, opened the oven door, put our clothes in, danced around shivering. Then we got dressed in our oven warmed duds. Aunty Bert came in with the milk. Uncle Joe did not like milking …. but that will be another story.

We looked out the window at the chicken house and Uncle Joe was coming back with the eggs. Something was following him. A big MOOSE! We hollered at Joe through the window. Joe looked up. The moose must have heard us because it turned and walked around the right corner of the chicken house.

When he came in we all told him at the same time. "Moose! Moose! Moose!"

He looked out the window. "Dares no moose dare".

He finally believed us, got out his hunting rifle, went outside and carefully snuck around the right corner of the chicken house. Nothing for a while. Then from the left side comes the moose. Moose stops and listens to the chickens through the windows. Joe shows up sneaking back through the snow.

We could see the moose and Uncle Joe approaching the corner. They get to the corner at the same time. The moose scares Uncle Joe. Uncle Joe scares the moose. Uncle Joe was so surprised that he didn't shoot the moose

Allan, Joanne Aunty Bert and Lynne

I don't know for sure where this part fits in. This is about Aunt Caroline, and her brother Jonas Walfredson when he first came from Sweden. The two of us were on the roof of the house where we were staying in Fraser Lake. We were fixing a roof that was leaking. He was saying words in Swedish and pointing at the objects, saw, nail, hammer, tar, roof. At another time he had been out fishing in the lake and came back absolutely white and scared. He was talking very excitedly in Swedish to my mom and Aunt Caroline about a big something he saw in the lake. He was slowly rowing the boat and the water was calm like glass. The something was big and alive and about the length of the boat. He could see large fins on its back. Aunty Caroline calmed him down and told him that this must have been a sturgeon. A BC lake, Okanagon, is said to have sea serpents. I bet that a sturgeon is what it is.

It seems all the time I spent in Vanderhoof was spent in Fraser Lake. However some things that happened in Vanderhoof were worth repeating.

In the winter of forty-seven, I had my own skates and went skating quite often with the Lewis boys on a creek about a hundred yards from the house. As the winter went on the water levels got lower and lower. The ice on the water would sink so that the middle of the creek was a lot lower than the sides. You could skate down hill to the middle of the frozen creek. One day, skating by myself something happened which could have been just terrible. While climbing out of the creek on this tilted old ice the ice broke and I fell through. I didn't land in water but in a space between ice layers. I hit the ice under me, slid some and broke through another layer. I kept sliding down until I was in water up to my chest. I rolled over on my back and slowly inched my way out by digging holes in the tilted ice with the back of the skate blades. This took a long time and after many rests I got out. By this time my soaked snowsuit had frozen solid. I could not get my skates off as the laces were frozen too. I picked up my gum boots and started walking home on my skates. This was a slow process. Too slow in fact because I had to do a number two… I didn't make it home in time. Mom was not at all pleased with me.

Grandpa came and stayed with us during this winter and spring. He would tell us the same Klondike Stories all over again. He showed us how cooking was done. His favorite meal was breakfast. He said you had to have a good breakfast and eat enough to last all day, just in case there was no more food until the next breakfast. He tried to get us to eat his breakfast but we, Larry was visiting, just sat wide eyed and watched him eat it. Here is what he had most mornings: Two pieces of buttered toast in the bottom of a big bowl, lots of cooked oatmeal on that, six big spoons of brown sugar, and Roger's Golden syrup poured over that. Finally he opened a can of Pacific Condensed Milk and poured most of it over everything in his bowl. Then he would eat the whole thing. All the time he would be groaning with delight, while the milk and syrup dribbled down his chin.

Mom was a practical joker and was always funning around. April Fool's Day was next day. We knew she would have something planned for this. We, Dad, Brian, Grandpa and I were ready for her. We weren't going to get fooled a bit. We were very quiet April Fools morning. Mom was making breakfast. Grandpa was tackling his bowl. Mom suddenly looks out the window and yells, "Moose! Moose! Moose! Lots of them!" We of course didn't look up from breakfast but sat and looked at our plates as she was jumping up and down waving her arms and trying to get us to look out the window. Of course we didn't. After awhile she said, "Oh gosh, they've gone." We didn't give her a chance to April Fool us!

A bit later I got my boots and coat and mitts on to go to school. Out in the yard in the fresh snow were hundreds of moose tracks and moose berries.

This moose pic was taken a lot
later at another house.

Here is another moose story. I went to school with a blonde girl. She lived south of town. One day her dad brought a baby moose home. The mother had been killed. The moose was raised by the young girl.

On a Saturday morning on the way to town I met her as she was going to the post office. She was holding a length of twine. On the other end of it was her huge ungainly moose. It was almost full grown. The moose was very timid and afraid of the big town and kept close to Georgina for protection. When she went into the post office the moose was told to stay outside. The poor thing climbed the wooden steps, opened the door with its nose and walked right in.

Our spring of 1948 was a late spring, and I was eight at the time. There had been lots of snow and this stayed around forever. Finally in late May the snow stopped, the sun came out, not warm but hot. The snow melted. Everything was water and mud. Vanderhoof is built on the Nechako River. The river started to rise and rise. The entire town was surrounded by water. Dad's planer mill was flooded completely. There was no way out of Vanderhoof until the end of June.

One evening in the spring of 1949 we were having a lazy time. Mom was out at a meeting. Dad was reading on the couch. Brian was playing with a neighbour boy, Harvey Kerr. He was our steady babysitter. I was playing with a model steam engine that Dad had bought me for Christmas. One put water in the boiler, alcohol in the burner and the wheels turned and the whistle blew. But this did not happen this time. I was laying beside the engine, flicking the drive wheel when, "BAM!" The lights went out for me. Brian was screaming. Dad had run over to see what was wrong with him. I was over in a corner. The engine had exploded and hit me in the face so I wasn't saying anything. The main part of the boiler had hit me square in the mouth.

The left side of my face was scalded. My mouth was real bad cut inside. Two front teeth had been broken off. I don't remember going to the hospital but I guess I must have. I did recover, all except the teeth. There was no dentist in Vanderhoof. In fact the teeth did grow and fill out. The explosion was blamed on Vanderhoof's hard well water. Now my dentist keeps asking me when do I want my teeth fixed. I am now 70 years old and figure that fixing them now won't improve my looks much…

Larry Dahlgren, Terrence Matthews, Beau,
Me, Ted Johannson, Billy Morley.
My Birthday, Robinson Beach

1950 was the year that Fraser Lake Sawmills was rebuilt. This was now a beautiful modern mill.

It was powered by steam. All the wood waste from the sawmill would provide fuel for the steam boiler. All Fraser Lake was proud of this wonderful planer mill. I asked, "Uncle Louie, how powerful is the steam engine?" I was thinking back to my steam engine at the same time running my tongue over my broken teeth. He said, "If the steam boiler ever blew up all that would be left of Fraser Lake would be a wet spot!"

On a Sunday, Dad, Mom, Brian and I went down the lake on a fishing trip. We caught maybe 18 trout. We started back at four or so. Returning, we pulled our boat out of the water at the mill. We walked with our fish up the hill and through the trees to Uncle Louie's house. Mom and Dad had gone further up the hill to Grandma Dahlgren's. I was outside with Larry.

A loud rumbling BOOM! We both looked down the hill. Wow! Look! Smoke was rising in the air like an atomic bomb cloud. The cloud was filling the sky and making it dark. Uncle Louie heard us from the kitchen. He came out, took one look and, "Yeesus the Mill's on fire!"

I ran up the hill to Grandma's screaming, "The mill's on fire! The mill's on fire!" Dad was in the outhouse. He came out running and pulling up his pants. We ran down out of the trees to see. The smoke was awesome. The noise was worse. Everyone was running, yelling, crying.

Mom took me to our Fraser Lake house where we were to stay the night with Anne Marie. The sky was all red. The crackling noise of the burning was terrifying. All I could think about was, "If the steam boiler ever blew up all that would be left of Fraser Lake would be a wet spot!"

Later that night Anne Marie came and told me not to worry. She took me out in the dark to look at the mill. All that was left was the hot hot glowing frames of the buildings.

I found out later that my cousins, Joanne, Lynne and Allan watched the mill fire all night. The Johnson farm was right across the lake from the Mill. They sat on the beach under a blanket until the last flames went out.

This was the end of our time in Fraser Lake. The mill had not been properly insured. Dad, Uncle Louie, Mr. Vinnedge and Mr. Lepoidevein lost all their money.

We moved to the coast.

Dad's mom was quite ill and for one summer we stayed in an auto court real close to the beach in White Rock. This was a wonderful vacation. There was swimming every day the sun shone and the sun was shining every day. White Rock beaches are very flat. At low tide the water is miles from shore. There is nothing but sand. In low parts there were pools with eel grass. In the grass lived big crabs.

The first time to the water, our dog Beau, a Labrador water dog ran and ran ahead of us to the water. He stopped when he was chest deep and started drinking. "Oh oh, this is not good!" The dog spent the rest of the day trying to keep Brian and I out of the water. He would grab our bathing suits with his teeth and pull us back out of that awful stuff. Later on he did let us go in. I guess he thought swimming and wading was all right as long as we didn't drink the stuff.

Grandma Engelson

We went south to Seattle to visit Grandma quite often. Dog Beau stayed back with the motel owners. Grandma Engelson lived in this big city.

I thought it was quite dirty. The air was "yellow" and smelled bad. I was told this was from the coal burning stoves and the manufacture of coal gas that was piped all over the city.

I developed a taste for "Curly Ice Cream Cones" as we didn't have any up in Canada. Grandma lived in the top half of a house. I guess you would call it a "walk-up flat". Her address number had a ½ attached to the end of it. She wasn't feeling too good. She had a very weak heart and stayed in bed most of the time.

I liked Uncle Vernon best. He had a car and we went out grocery shopping. We even could buy bread that was already sliced! It was called "Wonder Bread". After our grocery shopping we would go over to Boeings and watch all the planes. There were bombers, row after row as far as you could see. Mostly they were B17's and B29's. These were returning after the War. They were always landing and taking off.

This grandma was my favorite even though she lived far away. For my birthday and for Christmas she always sent me a pile of stuff and she seemed to know what kids my age would like.

My ninth Christmas present. I still have it
The jeep still works when you wind it up.

We got back from this first trip to the states and were welcomed by our dog Beau. He stayed outside our motel unit for the week we were gone and guarded the door. In fact he did such a good job that he didn't even let anyone dump our garbage can.

At the end of the summer we moved to Victoria.

Chapter Six

VICTORIA, SOUTH PARK ELEMENTARY SCHOOL

We came here because Dad's Aunty Rosie had cancer and her house was empty. When we opened the front door and went in Dad was amazed to see his rocking chair that was given to him when he was little. We still have the chair. I found a model of a steam train engine. It was about 4 feet long. We never did try to get it to work. My mouth and face were still tender from the last one and I kept thinking of the steam boiler in the Fraser Lake Mill Fire.

This house was across the street from Beacon Hill Park. The street out front was lined with large horse chestnut trees. In our back yard there was a walnut tree. The ravens would pick these nuts and fly over the paved streets and drop them to break them open. I liked Beacon Hill Park.

Dad took me down to the YMCA. He wanted to show me to a favorite friend of his. His name was Archie McKinnon. He was the top swimming coach in Victoria. We went down some stairs to the swimming pool. Dad found Archie in the large shower room. Everyone was naked except Dad and I. Dad introduced me to Archie and I shook his hand. All I could remember of him was the steam, his furry body and his private parts that were at my eye level. Later Archie taught me to swim. We had to swim with nothing on. That bothered me.

This was a wonderful place to hang out.
I liked the "Crystal" much better than the "Y".

I found the Crystal Garden Pool. Soon I was enrolled in South Park Elementary. My stay here was so short that I didn't have time to make any friends. My Uncle Bob lived in Victoria and had a daughter, Carol, who was my age but she was a girl.

I spent a lot of time in the old Provincial Museum. This was nothing like the one now. There were lots of stuffed animals. On the top floor there were many glass cases with stuff inside. There were lots of bugs on pins. I really liked the stuffed animals .

Last Saturday, October Oct 2nd, 2010. I took my son-in-law Graham and granddaughter Anna, to the museum in Victoria. To my wonder, they have recreated the old museum as a historical exhibit. There were all my old stuffed animal friends and of course all the bugs on pins!

Chapter Seven

NORTH VANCOUVER, LONSDALE ELEMENTARY

Before the year was out we moved to North Vancouver.

Dad had some injuries overseas from plane crashes. Also he was suffering from the effects of the war and the accident he had when in Pinchi. After we moved into a rented house in North Vancouver he spent a couple of months as an out patient at the military hospital in Vancouver called Shaughnessy.

I was soon enrolled in Lonsdale Elementary. We spent longer in North Van so I managed to make some friends. One was Billy Bissett. We had lots of fun together.

The best times were the winter. Snow would come down and down and the schools would close. Billy and I spent our time on sleighs exploring the hills. There were lots of them. We lived on twenty-fifth avenue. One day we found a way to sleigh ride all the way to Marine Drive without going on a main road.

My mom was alone a lot with me and brother Brian. The house we were in was very expensive to rent. In fact once Dad's big 1948 Desoto was towed away because he couldn't make payments. We did get it back.

Pic of Brian, me and Beau in North Vancouver

Chapter Eight

QUALICUM BAY, DASHWOODELEMENTARY

Dad did get some money together with the help of veterans affairs and we bought an Auto Court and Fish and Chip shop at Qualicum Bay on Vancouver Island. By now I was 11 and entered grade six at Dashwood Elementary which was ten miles from Qualicum Bay.

Because we had to go by bus to school I was able to find friends rather quickly. Again school wasn't that important. The time away was much better. Of course with the auto court, large house and fish and chip shop which also sold groceries we were all pretty busy. In fact, Grandma Dahlgren from Fraser Lake came to live with us to help. She looked after cleaning and bedding in the ten cabins.

Mom did cooking with Dad. He also did most of the shopping.

Every morning in the summer we, Dad and I, would go down to Deep Bay to get fresh cod. I peeled potatoes and potatoes and more potatoes. In between times I had to pack wood for the cabins. Most of the year the auto court was empty but on long weekends and the summer the place was filled. The beach across the road had good swimming and we had two boats with inboard engines for rental. In the summer a sack of potatoes had to be peeled before I could go down to the beach. I usually got help from Robbie or Leland.

I had to baby sit brother Brian. He was four now. He liked the beach and water a lot and could swim after a fashion.

NEW KID IN TOWN

Qualicum Bay Auto Court
Grandma Dahlgren and her cousins.
Also Brother Brian.

Even so, with all the work for everyone, in the winter time nothing happened. Dad had to go out and get a job. He found work running a gas donkey at a log dump in the Big Qualicum river. But here he got hurt. He got hit in the eye with something and had to go back to Shaughnessy.

Qualicum High School

At the beginning of September all the Dashwood sixes moved to Qualicum High in grade seven. This did not last long, as we had to move again.

The high school was on shift and us grade sevens had to take the afternoon shift, from 12:30 until 4:30. When I got off the bus, papers had to be delivered in the dark.

Well, with no work from Dad, the Auto Court was sold and we ended up a bit better because we then bought a house in North Burnaby.

Chapter Nine

NORTH BURNABY, ALPHA JUNIOR HIGH

This move happened in the Fall. Dad had a house picked out for us. This was in a nice neighbourhood.

Last year I did drive by our old house on 1440 Rosser Ave. It still looks the same.

Dad was still looking for work. We didn't have much money. But with lots of love in the house from Mom, Brian and I didn't notice so much.

I found out later that during this time our parents had to sell all Mom's gold jewelry for food and extras. Years later, when I found out about this my wife, Coral and I replaced most the jewelry as a thankyou.

Dad had to continue the treatments in the hospital. I was now in grade seven and almost 13. I got a paper route, bigger than the one on the island. This kept me in spending money. I became a city boy, traveling downtown on the street cars and going to movies on my own. Here we stayed for two years. My school was Alpha Junior High. This was a brand new school. Nothing was really finished.

My teachers here were mostly all good ones and I still remember the best ones.

After a year I wasn't called the new kid anymore. I found a job delivering newspapers. This supplied me with movie money. I bought some stuff. When we moved again I had enough saved up to buy a brand new Swedish bike.

This bike sure was much better than a CCM. (Canada Cycle Manufacturer) We called them "Canada's Craziest Make." My old bike weighed twice as much as the new Swedish one.

Something of note. During grade eight two kids from the school caught polio. One was a pretty girl from my class. She died. This did put a scare in everyone. Soon after the salk vaccine was ready. It was given to us in a drink.

My faithful companion , Beau, got sick and passed away.

Dad finally got a real job. He was a policeman again, like he was before the War. This time he was working away from home in a construction town called Kemano. This was the construction town for the power plant for the aluminum smelters of Kitimat. He worked for Alcan as part of their own Security Police. He was still trying to better himself as the "enforcing" in Kemano was pretty tough. There were too many fights between the international workers.

He applied for and got a better job. This was with the Federal Government as a Fisheries Inspector on the North Coast. He was to be based in Prince Rupert.

So, Dad went to Rupert and found a house. We, Mom, Brian and I, of course went back to Fraser Lake. I had just finished grade eight and summer was here. I was older now. I would be 14 in August.

I had a new bicycle. So when we arrived we had wheels of a sort. Larry and I biked all over.

We had a great summer. Uncle Louie was having a summer cabin built on a nearby lake called Francois, pronounced Frances. Larry and I stayed there. Dad lent us his small boat and motor. Uncle Louie gave Larry and I a whole drum of boat gas for use with this boat on the lake. The gas lasted us all summer. Uncle Louie told us that since we were thirteen this would be our last summer of freedom. We would be put to work next year to earn our keep!

At the end of August our family was on the way to Prince Rupert by train.

Chapter Ten

PRINCE RUPERT BO ME HI

Some Fishery Patrol Boats in Rupert

We saw our house. Not much. We lived downstairs. A young fisherman and younger wife stayed above us. He played nice accordian. Just about every night we could hear his music.

Rupert was the land of rain. There was no mud because all that got washed away a long time ago. There was just little trees and muskeg and then the docks for the fishboats and fish canneries. The town and all its houses and buildings were built on solid rock. All the fishing made this a busy place.

However, the rain dulled everything. To go to school I had to buy a raincoat, rainhat and rubber galoshes. Galoshes were rubber overshoes. You didn't use an umbrella because of the unending wind. An umbrella wouldn't last a day. Not very often could I use my bike to attend school.

The school was called "Bo Me Hi" This was short for Booth Memorial High School. When grades and reports were given I found out that I was not so dumb after all. After the first report card I started making friends.

I joined the Air Cadets. This kept me out of mischief most of the time. In fact by springtime I was selected to go down to Air Cadet camp in Chilliwack.

This meant buying all the gear needed: so many pairs of shirts, pants, socks and underwear. We were actually going to start learning to fly.

However, plans were put on hold. Dad got a promotion and we were going to be sent to Bella Coola. By this time the moves were getting to me. I was a bit depressed with this one. Ugh! What a name! This would mean more rain and fog. I would be further away from everything.

Chapter Eleven

BELLA COOLA
SIR ALEXANDER
MACKENZIE HIGH

I was completely devastated. I had friends in Rupert, was doing okay in school, and was really looking forward to go to Chilliwack to Air Cadet Camp. I was now 14 years old and girls were starting to look okay.

The morning of our trip looked like any other day in Rupert. The sky was grey, the hills were darker grey, the water was black and the rain was sideways... and still I didn't want to leave.

The trip from Rupert to this valley took a week by Union Steamship. The water was black, the sky was grey and the rain came down. The boat stopped at every place on the map. This trip could have taken a single day but we were on "Coast Time". At

Ocean Falls, a pulp and paper town, all our furniture, car, and us had to transfer to another Union boat. I watched our furniture being unloaded on the dock in the rain. We stayed at the Martin Inn for a few days waiting while the rain came down. My brother, Brian, who was seven, and I had one room and Mom and Dad had another. That first day the rain was coming down harder than in Rupert. The second day was worse than the first and on the third day we awoke to a steady roar. The clouds were on the sea. Rain was bouncing six feet off the planks on the dock. Is this a taste of what Bella Coola would be? Blah…

    The next day, May 12th 1954, dawned clear and warm. After a quick breakfast in the dining room I took Brian out on the boardwalk. Everything was bright. There were no clouds. I was amazed at the height of the mountains. Everything seemed new and much better than boring Rupert. This was going to be the start of a new adventure. I asked Dad if the mountains were going to be the same in our new town. He told me that the mountains would make the ones here in Ocean Falls look like little hills.

    Finally, the boat, the Catala, arrived and we watched our stuff being loaded. This was May 13th and another sunny day. Our furniture and our family, that is Mom, Dad, and young brother, Brian and

I left Ocean Falls for this valley with the peculiar name, Bella Coola.

I stayed out on deck for most of the 100 miles and watched the mountains grow and grow. As the mountains got larger the water, which was clear and dark, slowly changed to something that resembled grey green milk. I was told this colour was from the glacier melt water. The inlet had now closed into a steep narrow fiord. All the peaks had snow on them and narrow glaciers tumbled all the way to the valley floor. The mountain tops were so close you felt you could touch them. To look at the tops of those snowcapped peaks one had to look straight up.

The boat slowed as it approached our destination, a little dock and warehouse. A crowd of people could be seen on the dock.

I was quite surprised to see such a welcoming committee. Each week, on boat day, the entire valley came down to watch for anything new. This included passengers, tourist, supplies, and of course, new valley citizens.

Union Ship, Catala at Bella Coola

We would fit in pretty well in this town. Our last name, Engelson, was a Norwegian name and all the original whites were descended from Norwegian settlers.

Our house was a simple affair. This was white with green trim and surrounded by a white picket fence. Inside there was an office, bedroom living room, and bathroom all opening on a centre hall. Under the floor of this space was an oil furnace that heated the hall. On the ceiling above the furnace was a grilled vent which gave heat to the upstairs. This area top had two bedrooms, I was given the one on the east side. Brian had the bedroom on the West.

Later that first week I was in the back yard of our new place burning some packing boxes. Two boys came past the back fence to scout me out. They were Terry Brynildson and Larry Levelton. They didn't say anything, just walked by, and nodded. They of course would give the word to everyone else. "New kid in town!" Of all the places I had been this one turned out to be the easiest to make new friends.

The Monday after arrival, I caught the school bus for the trip 10 miles up the valley to Hagensborg, where the high school was located. Stepping on to the bus I was greeted by a grinning face under a huge cowboy hat. This was Daryl Smith who was to become a good friend.

The bell rang and our classroom slowly filled with the senior class, grades 9, 10, 11 and 12.

The teacher didn't even welcome me. He just looked at Daryl and said, "Take off your hat."

Daryl looked at him with his wide blue eyes. The entire class was giggling. Daryl said, "No."

The teacher who was the principal, said again with a deeper voice, "Take off your hat."

More supressed giggles. Daryl didn't say anything but slowly stood, turned around and reached up to remove his large stetson. The class was close to hysterics. Off came the hat.

The principal looked at Daryl in shock. "You may put your hat back on."

Daryl, it turned out had a contest with Billy Mecham as to who could go the longest without getting a haircut. Daryl , who had Afro hair, won and the older boys had given him a haircut. They had shaved his head, at least all the hair that was under the hat. Later on that morning, the janitor, Mr. Svisdahl, who was the local barber as well as the janitor, shaved off the remainder of Daryl's fuzzy hair.

This school, Sir Alexander Mackenzie High School, was the first school in the province that had full integration of the First Nations People. Of course we only referred to them as Indians.

Just two teachers looked after us, the senior classes that is.

Bella Coola town was just called the townsite. Years before everyone moved over from the nice side of the river, the northside, to the southside. The move was made because every Fall the river changed its course a bit and the northside got flooded. This southside was not as good a location because of the mountains. The sun did not shine directly in the town from October to March each year. Winters could get frightfully cold. But the ground was higher and the high water would not bother the town anymore.

Being in a small place like this meant things that a city kid took for granted just weren't there. Anyone who wanted electric lights had to go and buy a generator. There was no radio reception as the mountains stopped all signals from getting in except in the early morning. In 1954 there was no practical road out of the valley. Newspapers came in by boat once per week. There was no hotel, no cafe, only one grocery store, one gas station, and one general store to buy everything else.

So what was a boy like me to do? He went to school, worked at home, hung out with friends in their homes, read, daydreamed a lot, ate, and slept, but most importantly kept busy doing the things this generation doesn't seem to have time to do anymore. Stuff like exploring, hiking, bike riding, climbing, fishing, hunting, swimming, and skating. Hobbies, like building models, radios, furniture, and making old machinery work also kept us busy. Most everyone played some sort of a musical instrument. There was no such thing as someone on welfare

Dad also took us up the valley sometimes on his trips to check over the river. On one of these outings we had to go up to the top of the Bella Coola river system to the Atnarko River.

After a two hour walk we arrived at Bert Robson's place. Some called it a lodge, others said it was a ranch. We stayed for a couple of days. Bert was a big game guide and worked for dad as a Fisheries Guardian. Mr. Robson was a wonderful person to be around. He was a first war veteran and his house was filled up with souvenirs of the war and hunting trophies. Attached to each souvenir in his house was a story.

Mom, Brian and Bert

Everything was spotless. He did not have electricity in his house or running water. However, he did have an electric generator in a bunkhouse which was close to the house where his hunting clients stayed. A bathtub had been brought in on horseback.

The paying hunters had lights, hot and cold running water and did not have to go outside to visit the outhouse. Bert did not like all that stuff and preferred to live without those creature comforts.

Bert feeding some of his deer

Come to think about it, Bert had a large kerosene operated refrigerator in his kitchen. That too had to have come up on horseback. His yard, which was about 100 yards square, was a hay field and at this time all he had were 40 deer, which came down at night and could be seen in the morning. He did not hunt within 10 miles of his place. Once Bert woke me at daybreak to watch a couple of big bucks fighting in the morning fog. He had one special buck, which could drive the others away.

He taught my brother and me to shoot. As I said before, the house was a wonderful museum. One wall was covered with old guns, sabers, bayonets and other souvenirs from the First World War. He wouldn't let us shoot his elephant gun though. He told us that he got that while on Safari.

Our family would also go up in the Fall and fish for river run Cohoe. Bert was a very kind man and made all feel welcome.

Brian and I shooting at targets

That winter I had my first taste of Bella Coola's kind of winter. In the summer a West wind would come from the ocean.

I remarked to Darrel saying how strong the wind was. He just said, "Wait until the East wind starts."

This happens in the wintertime. The colder the temperature, the harder the wind blew. The more the wind blew the more the snow came. In a couple of days the town would freeze. The river would freeze over. Water lines would break. Snow would blow right through any crack. I would wake in the morning with snow blowing in around the window frames. This snow didn't melt in my room either. The bedroom window faced the East. This house had been built by the government. If someone from Bella Coola had built the house, windows or doors would not be built on the East side.

I told you of keeping busy. Now, I was fourteen in 1954, Our big adventure for this year was going to the Anahim Stampede. Anahim Lake was about 100 miles from the townsite. The group going consisted of Daryl Smith 14, Harvey Gilbert 14, Leslie Kopas 15 and me. Our parents must have had a lot of faith in what we were going to do or they were trying to get rid of us.

You must remember in that year there was no way out of the valley to the East except by foot or horse. A road was being built but was not ready for traffic yet. We spent a week planning the trip. What would we take? Sleeping bags, cooking gear, food, axes and knives. We wouldn't have to take a tent because of telegraph line cabins. Finally. in early July the day came.

Leslie's dad, Cliff Kopas had made arrangements for us to stay at Ike Sing's. Ike was one of British Columbia's few Chinese cowboys, maybe the only one. He was the propietor of this general store come trading post for Anahim. We were to bunk at his place.

On July 7th Mr. Kopas, took us to the end of the road. We shouldered our packs, some pictures were taken and we were off.

Daryl, Me, Leslie, Harvey leaving
from Young Creek

Our route would follow the old telegraph trail. Our group couldn't really get lost as this telegraph line was in use and was the phone line to civilization. The walk would be 55 miles, Young Creek to Anahim. There were two "cabins" on the way used by line repair men or anyone else who needed shelter.

After a short walk of 4 miles we checked in to Bert Robson's where we were fed. Mr. Robson knew that teenagers were always hungry. Little did we know but that would be our last real meal until returning to Bert's a week later. Food you cook for yourself over a campfire really doesn't count. From Atnarko to the Stampede would take us three days.

We did not stay overnight at the Robson place as we, Daryl, Les, Harvey and I, were anxious to get started. After some juice, good byes and good wishes we were off. The first of the two line cabins was our destination

We reached the "log cabin" about 9 PM. This was not much of a place. There were two log bunks against the back wall, a small air tight stove for heat and cooking, a log bench and a crude table. The place smelled of its usual residents, pack rats.

We flipped a coin to see who got the bunks. Leslie and I lost and decided to sleep outside as the ground was softer than the floorboards inside.

This sleep under the "stars" lasted until midnight. We woke with rain drizzling down through the big trees. Dragging our bags inside we were greeted by, "I told you so."

A couple of hours later I woke with a strange sensation. An object of some sort was on my stomach. This object then walked to my chest. I could smell it. A pack rat! I whispered, "Les!" He whispered, "I know. They're all over!" Carefully he got a match out of his pocket. The rat on my chest was joined by another. "These things must be tame," I thought. I got my hand on a piece of firewood. Les whispered, " One, two, THREE!" and struck the match on the floor. I threw the piece of firewood at a rat scrambling out of the light. In the glare of the match we could see dozens of the varmints.

Needless to say we didn't get much sleep and got an early start in the morning. Harvey cooked some pancakes of a sort. We ate, packed the dishes dirty and were off in the half light of dawn. 14 year old boys really didn't like to do dishes.

Lunch stop was at a place called Sugar Camp. This was on the junction of the Hotnarko and the Atnarko rivers.

We kind of did the dishes there. Soon we were walking and climbing through the Atnarko Canyon.

The next line cabin was above Precipice twenty-two miles away. This place, Precipice, is where the telegraph trail goes from the coast forest of large fir and plenty of water to the interior plateau of small jackpine and little water. Precipice was an almost vertical line of cliffs formed from basalt. We arrived at Precipice in the afternoon. Jack Weldon's Ranch was at the foot of this escarpment. Getting close we could see the main cabin and a few outbuildings. Someone could be seen running away through the trees. Jack Weldon welcomed us. We asked Mr. Weldon about the boy we saw. Jack explained that the boy was his son and was a bit leery of strangers. He had been raised there at Precipice. He wouldn't come back until we had left. Jack was told that we would be back in about a week.

We started up the trail, which was quite a climb with our packs. This was a strange trip as the bottom was a moist warm west coast summer and the top was a dry cool interior spring. There was lots of space between the trees on top and the trail was so faint at times that the telegraph line was needed to point the way. By late evening we arrived at the line cabin. We figured it was placed there because there was a small stream so water wouldn't be a problem. Canned beans were served for supper. We got a pot of water from the creek and climbed into our sleeping bags. Our sleep was much better, no rats...

Frost greeted us in the morning. This was the first week of July. We had our usual breakfast of pancakes and eggs.

Leslie cooked this time. I had to do the dishes. I went over to the tiny stream with the pots and... no water... the stream had dried up over night. We scraped the pots and dishes with sand and put them away again, dirty. We promised that we would clean them when we found water.

There were only 20 miles left. A couple of hours later a small trickle was found crossing the trail. We used that water with some sand and got most of the stuff off the dishes and were on our way again. No mothers to worry about, we were free!

And on we went. Leslie figured that we had a couple of more miles to go. Hours later we were still walking. Had we missed Anahim Lake? We didn't want to go to Williams Lake. But still the telegraph poles stretched out through the little pines. Finally, a dog, and then an Indian kid, then a small log cabin. We had made it! We stopped to clean up a bit. We wanted to make an impression on the town. We also wanted to make sure that we looked like locals instead of tourists. We all wore jeans. We had proper western shirts. These had been purchased at the Kopas store. Daryl and Harvey always wore big stetson hats so we thought that if Les and I stayed close to them we all could pass as locals. Half an hour later we walked passed another cabin and then another.

In front of us was a larger log building with a covered porch. 3 horses were tied to the hitching rail out front. Anahim Lake!

We walked up to the horses. Two Indians and two whites were leaning against the front and gave us the once over. Each had big western hats, snap button shirts, skinny jeans and of course cowboy boots.

"You must be the boys from Bella Coola, We was expectin' you," said one old cowboy. "Ike Sing will be back in a while." Quite a downfall thinking we could blend in with the scenery. What gave us away? Two things. We were walking. Cowboys can't walk for long in their boots. And most important, we came from Bella Coola, where the sun shines for a few months each year. In Anahim the sun shines everyday or thereabouts. Us kids were all a pasty white. Anahim Whites were the same colour as the Indians, at least their hands and faces.

Soon Ike Sing comes in. He was shorter than us with a round moon face and big smile. He wore a big western hat and large round thick glasses. "Welcome!" he said with a smile. Turning, he looked us over and saw Leslie who was the tallest and oldest, "You must be Leslie. Your father told me to see that you behave yourself."

Harvey, Daryl and I introduced ourselves and Ike took us next door to our accommodation, the bunk house. This was a one room log cabin containing one old brass bed, a stove, wash stand, table and some chairs.

"Make yourself comfortable. Oh, by the way. Some of my hands might drop by this evening but it is unlikely being stampede time and all." And Ike went back to the store.

After unpacking, we flipped for the bed. Leslie and I got that. The others claimed places to unroll their sleeping bags. We went back out to the store to see if there was a place to eat in town. Nope, out of luck again. Back to the bunk house where a meal was made on the kitchen stove with our canned beans.

After dinner time Daryl and I went off to the stampede grounds. Stampede was to start the next morning but ran on "Indian time". Indian time meant that it started after awhile... Besides the stampede corral there was a new building going up. This was going to be the dance hall. The whole thing had been built in a couple of days by some of the locals. This was built out of rough lumber. The floor was rough wood as well. How is anyone going to dance on that? Daryl and I soon found out as we were handed two hand planes and started smoothing the floor. This was going to take awhile. A few hours later we were given a break as some of the locals thought that this planing looked like fun. We left for the bunk house, Leslie and Harvey were cooking some more food from the store. I'm not too sure what we ate as all this happened over fifty years ago.

However, that night I well remember. What happened then I never did tell to my parents. In fact I don't even know if I should write it down. What the heck. It was all long ago.

I was pretty tired but decided to take a last walk around. In the distance and coming closer we could hear blood curdling screams and the sound of horses galloping full out.

The Stick Indians were coming in.

I will digress here for a moment. What is a Stick Indian? A Coast Indian lives on the coast and they have their own way of life, living in villages, getting their livelihood from the sea, either by fishing or working in canneries. The Stick Indians, Stickine , or Chilcotins are of a different language group and for the most part live in tents. The Coast Indians call these Chilcotins, Stick Indians because they come from the place of little jack pine trees or sticks. A group of them would come down to Bella Coola and live in an encampment in between the Indian Village and the townsite each summer They would trade homemade leather goods for food, eulachan grease, old clothing and some money. What I remembered best about them was the smell of their camps. This was the same smell as their fresh tanned leather gloves, shirts and moccasins and brought back memories of the Fraser Lake Indians. The men hunt and trap and ride horses. Many of them work as cowboys for the white ranchers, guides and packers. The women setup tents, cooked, tanned leather and made moccasins, gloves and other clothing from the moose and deer hides. They went wherever the men wanted to hunt, trap or work.

Going back to the story, The Indian men were arriving on horseback. The women and kids, on horse drawn wagons, had arrived earlier or were still coming. Some of the men had ridden all the way from Williams Lake Stampede which was over 200 miles away.

These were real cowboys. Most were local Indians who had a few dollars to spend for an entry fee.

Different societies have different ways of showing off, or strutting their stuff. These Indians showed us how well they could ride and were very proud of their mounts. At this time there were still some herds of wild horses. An Indian who wanted one could go and catch an animal, break it and tame it. Some animals we saw weren't very far from being wild. This racing, showing off, buying and selling happened each night during stampede. Most participants were well fortified with booze. We were offered some but I don't remember any of us taking any. As I have told you before, we were only 14 and customs were different back then.

With the wild horses and Indians and whites making about as much noise as possible our little group from Bella Coola turned in. We were very tired, having a full day of walking and a late night. Leslie and I were soon fast asleep in our sleeping bags on the big brass bed.

Suddenly I woke. Someone had just jumped on the bed. Some two had just jumped on the bed. Giggling and laughing both male and female, I was so scared I didn't say a word or move. I was on the bottom of a pile which was moving. All stopped…

A rough voice, "What the hell is this! Who the hell are you?"

I told him in a small voice, "It's only me." That didn't help. I was rudely shaken down to the bottom of the sleeping bag, dragged off the bed. Bump! Dragged to the door, out the door, Thump! The door shut. I decided I should not go back in there. A short time later the door opened again and Thump! another sleeping bag was tossed out.

This turned out to be Leslie. We made ourselves comfortable under the eaves of the bunkhouse and tried to sleep until morning.

I was first up. The two cowboys, a John Bragg and his friend, were pretty nice to us kids and apologized, not realizing that we were "guests". No mention was made of the girl voices we had heard.

Later that day a girl from Bella Coola showed up having hitched a ride from Vancouver. Her name was Jeanette Brynildsen. She was about 18.

I don't know where she slept during stampede time but it wasn't in the bunk house. She did take pity on us "children" and if she was around we did eat after a fashion. She was a good cook for canned stew and canned beans. At least she didn't burn them. Jeanette even washed our socks once.

Jeanette watching the rodeo. Dance hall is in the background

Now the rodeo business would start. Wild horses to be broke, Steers and bulls to ride, horse racing, and drinking. I think more attention was taken to drinking than anything else. Not much attention was given to winning or losing.

In the morning Harvey and I managed to rent two horses from some Indians that were camped close to the bunkhouse. We got the pair for twenty-five cents for the day. My horse had a wonderful saddle covered in tanned grouse feathers. This made for a nice soft seat. Harvey and I swung up on the saddles trying to look experienced. These were the first horses either one of us had ever been astride. How do you make them go? Giddyap! kick, kick kick! Nothing worked. After a half an hour of this we led them back because we couldn't make them go at all. The boy that had rented them saw us and laughed. The pair were a team! Harvey's was on the right and mine was on the left. The grinning Indian just moved my horse to the left side and put Harvey's on the right and everything was just okay. My horse was the lead horse and Harvey's horse went wherever my horse was going.

Me and the two-bit horse

We got our horses over to the stampede corral about nine in the morning. The entertainment had already started. Steer riding, bulldogging, saddle bronc and bareback bucking. Bragg had entered the steer riding but picked the wrong steer. It bucked him off straight over the horns and broke his nose on the way by. I saw him later on. He was smiling a lot and was having trouble walking. On the last day they had a wild cow race which turned out to be the most dangerous event of all. Two cowboys had to saddle a milk cow, fill up a beer bottle with milk and stay on the cow for a period of time. The day slowly wound along. There was a concession of sorts that sold pop and hotdogs. I couldn't afford either one of those. A cowboy called Pan Phillips was the cook. He kept hollerin' "Hot Doags, Hot Doags" We used that for our personal greeting for the next few days.

That night was when the new dance floor we had helped to plane the slivers off would get its first workout. We knew what Friday night dances were like from the dances in Bella Coola. They were not like this one. In Bella Coola every other Friday there was a dance in the Lobelco Hall. (Lower Bella Coola) This was half way between townsite and Hagensborg. One room was put aside for coats and babies. There was a stage for the dance band, a dance floor for dancing and a parking lot for drinking. There was no beer or wine in the hall, in bottles that is…

This structure in Anahim was just one large room with benches along the walls and a small raised area for the "band". The band consisted of one Indian and a small accordian. He knew one song and he kept playing it. Wednesday night, Thursday night, Friday night and Saturday night he played the same tune. He was only given a break when one of the white cowboys played a banjo. The Indian's song is still in my head. "Dancin', romancin', always on the go. Sun shining down on old Mexican Joe." These were all the words that anybody knew. Over and over and over again. The dancing never stopped. Cowboys and Indians pushing the women from one end of the floor to the other. Everyone wearing cowboy hats and boots. The place was packed. One could hardly see across the hall with the smoke and the few lights created with a small gas generator. The smell of rye whisky was thick in the air. "Dancin, romancin, always on the go. Sun shining down on old Mexican Joe!" Most of the cowboys were drinking hardstuff from mickeys or small flasks. These were replenished from time to time from outside.

A fight started. The fighters and most of the dancers, went outside for awhile, had some more drinks and come back in. By daybreak our group had enough and we went back to the bunkhouse, hoping that we wouldn't have to sleep outside again.

The next day was cold and clear with frost on the ground. After some pancakes, Daryl and I walked over to the Stampede grounds. Nothing doing there. The cowboys started showing up about noon. Everyone worked on "Indian Time". The third day of riding started at 2 in the afternoon.

I've left out some parts here and there, but the rest of the time in Anahim was similar, except everyone but us had hangovers. A couple of good snorts got the older boys ready to ride again.

One event occurred before we started back down to Bella Coola brought us back to reality. Something happened to Harvey. He got into an argument with one of us, I forgot who. He pulled a knife and didn't come back to Bella Coola with us. We heard later that he went south and later joined the army. Anahim Lake was connected to Williams Lake and the rest of the world by two hundred miles of dirt road.

Well, it came time for us to head for home. We had run out of money and food too. We didn't tell Ike Sing or anyone else for that matter. We left at eleven. Daryl had a half a pack of cigarettes, and a pack of chewing gum. This was all we had to eat until we got back down to a promised meal at Precipice.

Our packs didn't weigh much. All we had now were our sleeping bags, some pots 'n pans, and dirty clothes. We stopped for a rest at the line cabin, 22 miles out of Anahim, only six miles to Precipice and Jack Weldon.

I decided to run the last bit. I trotted along in the twilight and then in the dark, running over the trail and down the hill with my pack bouncing on my shoulders. I collapsed against the wall of the Weldon place. An hour later the rest of the troop, Daryl and Leslie showed up and decided that two in the morning was not the time to disturb the sleepers.

In the morning Jack invited us in. He offered us some pork and beans that had been bubbling on his stove. The aroma coming from the pot told us not to eat. It was rotten! We made excuses that we just weren't that hungry and left with our stomachs growling, thinking food food food with every step.

From here the road was all down hill. Billie Mecham and Jeanette Brynildsen passed us on horses in Atnarko Canyon. At four we arrived at Bert Robsons and helped Bert cook a great meal. We tried not to show how hungry we were but Leslie made a mistake and took a whole bunch of mashed potatoes and a mouthful of gravy and tried to swallow without chewing. Don't ever try that. Do what your mom says and chew your food before swallowing...

After helping Bert do the dishes we were on our way again. Seven miles later, at the end of the trail, my Dad picked us up with his old blue Plymouth. Bert had a radio telephone.

Well, this completes this little adventure. Our parents thought this was just a little "holiday" and now we could get to work supporting ourselves.

I told you that I was 14. That did not mean I couldn't work. I don't mean paper routes and delivering groceries and stuff like that. Most of the boys left school for work on fishing boats or in the bush logging at 15 or 16. The girls left at the same time for other reasons.

One day I was sent on my bike to the co-op for some groceries, I heard a holler, "Hey, Monte!" I skidded to a stop turned around and biked back to Blondie Stroud. He asked me if I wanted to make some money. I was then made an employee of the Bella Coola Waterworks and had to dig a 100 yard ditch to connect the town's water system with a new building that was to be the town's first bakery. $1.25 per hour. Wow! I never had so much money. On Friday Blondie came and looked at the ditch. He couldn't believe that I was about finished. He told me that every other ditch dug in town had to go through gravel and big boulders. All that was in my little ditch was fine sand.

At the end where the water line was to tie into the townsite system I had to dig down another 4 feet to get pipe wrenches to work. At the very bottom of this hole I found a strange iron blade stuck in a driftwood log. This object was made out of iron, seven inches long and still had an edge. In fact I still have it. It has some Chinese characters on it and a bumble bee. You try and figure out how that blade got there.

Chinese rice sickle found at Bella Coola

After this Blondie thanked me, paid me and told me he had another ditch for me to dig starting the next Monday.

Next Monday, early morning, 4:00 AM, I heard Dad leave to go out on Fisheries Patrol. A half hour later he came back and told me he fired the cook for being too drunk to walk. I heard later that he sobered the cook by throwing him off the dock. So I was no longer a ditch digger–I was now a "deckhand/cook". I told Dad that the only thing I had cooked before were pancakes. Mom gave me a cookbook. I packed some clothes into my sleeping bag, got hugs and kisses from her and was off. My pay was to be $237.00 per month after taxes. Wow! Dad fibbed for me and said I was 16 so the federal government would pay me.

This boat, named the Comrade II, was a charter boat, and didn't even come with an owner/skipper. This was just the boat, about 40 feet in length. Our hired skipper was Mr. Buce, I just called him Cap.

I was the rest of the crew and had to go where dad told us to go. We were to work out of Bella Coola and the big town of Ocean Falls. Ocean Falls had a regular fisheries vessel called the "Bonila Rock". Its crew was a Fisheries Inspector, Harry Grainger, a cook-deckhand, an engineer and a skipper.

During the course of the summer I got to see every foot of every waterway: North Bentinck, South Bentinck, Dean Channel, Burke Channel, Kimsquit, Kwatna, Cousins, and Cascade. When not cooking or deckhanding I went with Dad on his stream inspection trips, met lots of fishermen, boat crews, and bears. For fun we shot seals and sea lions. I found out later that this shooting was part of our job to keep the seal populations down. Dad gave five dollars for every seal nose turned in to him.

This "work" lasted until the middle of September, even though school started two weeks before. I was now fifteen and in grade ten.

I guess by now you have noticed that life was not at all boring in Bella Coola. School could have been but Daryl and I did enough in between times to make up for it.

Just after school started I was searching through our reading material which included the Eaton's catalogue and came across "Jew's Harp", 15 cents each. I ordered six dozen and sold them at school for 25 cents apiece.

Soon the school principal had confiscated most of these little musical instruments. He did give me a lecture on the proper place to practice "free enterprise."

This was the beginning of our grade 10 year. A good start.

Dad bought a piano for mom because she liked to play a bit. Since this instrument was in the house I started taking classical piano lessons from a Mrs

Mercer. After a couple of lessons she stopped me and said, "You really don't like this do you?" I told her I would like to play dance music. She hollered, "Richard. I have a student for you." Richard, was Mr. Mercer. He was an excellent piano player. Soon I was playing proper music for Bella Coola.

After Christmas Dad asked me if I wanted to try another season as a cook/deckhand on a different boat. This was to be in Rivers Inlet. I said yes. At the end of the school year I packed my sleeping bag and some clothes. Mom found my cookbook. She kissed me goodbye and I was off again.

The fisheries boat, the Bonila Rock, was waiting at the dock. I found out that I was going to be the cook on that boat for a few days on the trip to Rivers Inlet.

Boy, are those Fisheries' crews spoiled. I had to put out a tablecloth for lunch and dinner.

At my first breakfast I learned very quickly about boat superstitions. I put out the coffee, some sugar and a can of Pacific Milk. The engineer, Alex, who was about 4 foot six, saw the milk can and switched from his scottish brogue to pure Gallic and in one motion grabbed the can and hurled it. I ducked and the can went straight out an open porthole. I had opened the can upside down!

Before reaching Ocean Falls I learned about another superstition. I was on deck whistling my favorite tune from Anahim Lake. I was stopped by the deckhand. He said, "Don't you dare whistle. It will bring bad luck. That is how you whistle up a wind. If Alex heard you he would treat you like that milk can!"

At a cannery, Namu, I transferred to another boat, the Egret Plume and was on my way again. The next day, Sunday, we arrived at Dawson's Landing in Rivers Inlet where I met my new skipper and my home for the summer, the Corvette.

This "Corvette" was a green gillnetter, only 31 feet long. Its friendly engine was a 2 cylinder Easthope This green, oil covered contrivance made its presence known taking up half our living area. When running it was, "Kabut kabut kabut kabut". Easthope was the heater for the boat. When I was cooking it was a good place to balance our cooking pot. Its large flywheel at its front made a good seat.

There was a triangle forward where the two sleeping bags were stowed. All our clothes were in two canvas "duffel bags". The kitchen was a drop down table on the starboard side. When this was opened we had a one burner gas stove. You could not stand up in any place under cover except the wheel house.

Our food was kept in the main hold. For meals I sat on the aforementioned flywheel. The skipper/owner was a very nice grand father figure. Ray LaMarsh was his name. He had the same build as Santa Claus, with white hair but no beard.

Dawson's Landing was to be our base for the weekends. It was a very busy summer town composed of a couple of stores built on barges and lots of floats for the many hundreds of fishing boats. These docks were all tied to the shore behind an island to protect them from the summer storms. The fisheries inspector, Pat Sim, had a permanent house on the shore which was reached by a planked railed boardwalk. This building was very pretty, painted red and white like a lighthouse.

Speaking of paint. Apparently the fisheries had lots of paint. When there was nothing to do, out would come a can of paint. Our colour was green: green Corvette, green engine, green rowboat, green oars, The only part of the Corvette that wasn't freshly painted green was the bottom. But we pulled the boat out of the water once and painted that with copper paint.

Our job was not to ferry a fisheries inspector, but to patrol the fishing boundary which ran across the inlet. Rivers Inlet had the largest sockeye fishing run on the north coast. When the fish were getting ready to go up the Owikeno River gillnetters from all over the coast came to harvest the crop.

Ray told me to cook up a big lunch as today, Sunday, was the start of fishing season and we would be too busy for a proper supper. We left Dawson's surrounded by more fishing boats than I had ever seen.

Many other fish camps were in the area, all filled with gillnetters. Goose Bay, Duncanby, Goodhope, Whadams, Rivers Inlet, Kildala, and others with no names. Besides the independent boats, many were from Rupert. Hundreds came up from the Fraser River.

MONTE ENGELSON

A sailing gillnetter

Song of the Sockeye

Oh, hark to the song of the sockeye
Like a siren's call of old
When it gets in your blood you can't shake it
It's the same as the fever for gold

There's a hole in the BC coastline
River's Inlet's the place I mean
And it's there you will find the old-timer
And also the fellow who's green

NEW KID IN TOWN

Oh, the boats head for there like the sockeye
And some are a joy to the eye
While others are simply disasters
And ought to be left high and dry

Now, they go to the different canneries
And before they can make one haul
It's three hundred bucks for net, grub and gas
Which they hope to pay off before fall

Then it's off to the head of the inlet
At six o'clock, Sunday night
But when morning comes and you've got about three
The prospects don't look very bright

Of course, there is always an alibi
To account for a very poor run
The weather is wrong, the moon's not full
Or the big tides will help the fish to come

Now some of us think of the future
While others have things to forget
But most of us sit here and think of a school
Of sockeye hitting the net

And when the season is over
And you figure out what you have made
You were better off working for wages
No matter how low you were paid

So hark to the song of the sockeye
Like a siren's song of old
When it gets in your blood you can't shake it
It's the same as the fever for gold

Written by Ross Cumbers in 1939

In 1940 there were ten canneries in Rivers. Now, in 1955 only two remained, Whadams and Goose Bay. The sockeye were transferred from gillnetters to large collectors boats to still larger faster boats, called packers. These were filled with ice for a quick journey to bigger and more efficient canneries.

We arrived at the boundary which was an invisible line that stretched between large triangle markers set on each side of the inlet. This boundary was about 2 miles across. No boat was allowed to put a net in the water until 6 PM Sunday when the Egret Plume would give the signal. The boats could fish until 6 PM Friday. Boats were continually moving, jockeying for a better position and most were trying to be on the line at six. You have to understand that in a deep inlet on the coast the tide is always pushing the water in and out. In each 24 hours one would have two high tides and two low tides. The smart ones held back as there was not enough room for all of them on the line. The entire inlet was filled with these small gill netters.

Finally the signal was given. It was a large mortar shell. The smoky plume rose into the sky and BOOM, a fireworks pinwheel appeared high in the early evening sky just like the ones you could see at a fireworks display. All the boats put their throttles on high and roared around, dumping part of their nets overboard and allowing the water to pull the rest off the boat. Each net was 1200 feet in length. It had floats on the top and lead weights on the bottom.

Most gill netters looked like this

The newer boats had a gillnet wheel to store the net and power to bring the net back in. The older boats just had a pile of net on the aft end.

What was our job? For awhile I thought that it was just to yell at fishermen. Nets got run over. Other nets were set across others. The wind was blowing in with large waves and the tide was moving out. Some fishermen were told to pull up by big Ray LaMarsh as they drifted across the boundary line. To me I couldn't see how any fish would be caught. Too much confusion and we in our little boats were to keep order? Ha.

Soon it was dark. The fishermen exchanged the flag on the end of their nets with a floating oil lantern. Each boat had a white light on the mast so you could tell where the boat was. The nets were invisible in the dark. More nets got run over by more boats. What a mess!

To make matters worse. Ray said to me, "Monte, you take over, I'm, going to get a bit of shuteye. I think you will be all right. You've got a man's voice and no one can see you in the dark."

Well I stayed up running the boat from here to there and yelling at fishermen just like Ray did. About 2 AM Ray woke up and took over until breakfast time.

In the early morning light I could see that the boats were now behaving themselves. No more tangles and most were hauling in loads of Sockeye salmon. This was to be a good year.

Daytime was spent "kabupping" from one boat to another. We had to keep a rough tally on how many fish were being caught. The Corvette motored around showing the government flag. We would visit the canneries and fishing floats and talk to the fishermen. In fact, all week was like this. We would have an easy sleepy day and not much sleep during the nights.

Killer whales visited us to share in the fish. When they showed up no fish could be caught. One weekend while tied up in Dawsons Landing a large school of these beautiful animals came by. They were all jumping clear of the water and so close you could see them looking at you. A large white shark was hauled up in one net and left on a fish float. Everyone had to come and see it.

There were three big fish processing companies on the coast, BC Packers, Canadian Fish and Nelson Brothers. These owned many company boats which were leased by those who didn't have boats of their own. Some fishermen were as young as my 15 years. Large packer boats flying the company flags towed long lines of these small boats to the head of the inlet.

There were too many boats to count. I heard that year there were three to four thousand. Population of Bella Coola was about one thousand while the summer population of Rivers Inlet was close to ten thousand. Nelson Brothers had one line of boats without any engines, just oars and sails.

While all this was going on another group, a different sort of fishermen were clustered behind the boundary lines. These were called "Sports Fishermen". Rivers Inlet was known as the Spring Salmon Fishing Capital of the world. These Spring are sometimes called, Tyee, Chinook or King. All refer to the same fish. Many large boats, mostly American tourists, came here to fish each year. These fishermen would stay on larger yachts and fish from small boats. Some large boats stayed all season. New fishing crews would be flown in once per week from Seattle. The Fisheries Department ran a weigh-in station right at Rivers Inlet Cannery (RIC). We saw the largest fish every caught here on rod and reel, 86 pounds. These fishery guys used to tease me because of the bit of peach fuzz I had on my chin...

When the mortar rocket was sent up to end the weeks' fishing, the inlet emptied as all the gill netters headed in to a dock to repair nets and replenish supplies. Net wharves were provided by the fish companies. All nets were taken off the boats and checked for damage and repaired.

The Corvette and other charter boats like us moved in to the Fisheries Station at Dawson's Landing. Besides the stores for shopping, the fisheries had their own float with washrooms containing showers and clothes washing facilities. A fresh water line came from ashore. A woodburning stove heated the water which was stored in a hot water tank. Clothes were washed with a "wash board" and a lot of energy provided by me.

A wash board and tub

Looking back on this time it is hard to believe that 1955 was the last big catch of sockeye salmon in Rivers Inlet. Over one million fish were landed. Now they don't even allow any gillnetters in the inlet.

I had a camera with me but didn't take many pictures. Only one photo has survived. This was taken from the wheelhouse of the Corvette and shows a single fisherman who was tired of the rush at the boundary line and was pulling in a set near the open pacific.

I got some more pictures from the internet but could not find any that would actually show the amount of boats and people involved with the harvest. When the season opened on that first Sunday night one could imagine walking from one boat to another all the way across the inlet.

This picture shows a line of fishing dorys being towed out by a packer.

A fisherman on a net float checking over his gill net.

At summers end the fish had gone up the rivers and lakes to spawn. The fishing boats had gone home. The Fisheries put everything away for next year. I said goodbye to Ray LaMarsh at the cannery, Namu. The Bonila Rock took me to Ocean Falls and Dad's boat, the Comrade II had us back in Bella Coola on August 31st. This was my 16th birthday. Some friends made their way to our house for some cake. Elsie Gilbert gave me a little match box car. "My first car" she said. During the summer the Bella Coola students had worked for the Fisheries, fish companies, canneries, forestry and logging. They had left as kids and come back as adults.

One boy, Orville Rindero was drowned out on the open ocean. The troller he was crewing went down. The skipper drowned too.

School wouldn't be the same anymore.

Grade 11 passed rather quickly. We still took the bus to Hagensborg every morning for school. We had a new principal, Mr. Loosmore, who with his wife taught all the senior classes.

I soon got my driver's licence and was driving the family car around.

One day I upset Dad when I came home with an old motorcycle. $150 was the total cost.

Dad told me in no uncertain terms that I could not ride that bike. "They are dangerous!"

"You rode one when you were young"

"That's how I know they are dangerous!"

I had to give back the old Harley and get my money back

In the winter of 1955, one of Bert's hunter friends gave him a World War II Army Jeep. This vehicle was in California. Bert had to go out by the Steamship to Vancouver, take a bus to California and drive the jeep back. Only thing the hunter friends didn't realize was that Bert didn't have a licence. Where he lived you just didn't need one. No roads. Somehow he got back and learned how to drive through traffic on the way to Vancouver. The Jeep was placed on the Union boat. Upon arriving in the valley Bert drove it up from the docks, to the townsite. He stopped to see us and show off his new jeep. Before leaving for his home at the head of the valley he bought a case of dynamite. He used that to blast some rocks out of the way so that he could get his new vehicle to the Ranch.

I got my driver's licence in 1956. Dad sold me his car for $150.00 as I had made a lot of money in the last two summers working on fisheries boats in Bella Coola and Rivers Inlet. The Department of Fisheries supplied him with a government vehicle, a brand new 56 Land Rover! Our first trip in this was to go up to the end of the valley and try out Bert Robson's new road. While there I taught my 8 year old brother to drive on the deer pasture. Little Brian was so short that to start or stop he had to slide down and put his head on the bottom back of the seat to reach the pedals. We didn't tell Mom.

That winter we went back to the Robson place, Bert had gone and got himself married to an Indian lady called Josephine. Mom and her hit it off pretty good because mom could speak her language. Mom learned it from the time spent in the north amongst the Indians. Mom was quite surprised that she could understand Josephine.

I was asked if I wanted to go out on the trapline with Mr. Robson. Mom and Dad and my brother stayed behind with Josephine. Bert and I left through the snow. We were wearing our winter clothes and had "mukluks" on our feet. My mukluks were mom's that she wore when in Fort Nelson. Mukluks were moose hide moccasins that came up to our knees and would keep the snow out. Bert said that we wouldn't have to use snowshoes as the trail was firm. On the trapline Bert showed me how to bait the traps and snares. We got a few weasels and a mink. However, most of the traps were empty because something big had eaten the animals when they had been caught. Bert showed me tracks and said that a pair of cougars had been busy there. After resetting a trap he told me to stop and signaled me to be quiet. He took the safety off his rifle and went off the trail and told me to follow him. He showed me another trail made by the two cougars. He finished setting the traps and we were back to the lodge for food before dark and then it was time to go home.

That spring Bert and Josephine, with their green jeep, showed up at our house at the Townsite. I was away at school so was very surprised on my return to see spread all over our living room their entire winter's fur catch. There were the usual weasels called ermine, mink, and funny minks with orange throats, called martins. There was one beautiful lynx and two cougars. The smallest, the female had been caught in a trap, and skinned very carefully so that it could be mounted whole. He told us that it had already been sold to an American hunter. The largest cougar was skinned out flat. Bert said it measured eight foot two inches from the tip of its nose to the tip of its tail. I measured it later and it wasn't that big. It must have shrunk when he tanned it.

In our living room surrounded by the furs Bert told us this story…

Joesephine, Bert and winter furs

"After you left Atnarko the cougars got braver. Each morning Josephine and I would go out and try and beat the cats to the traps but all that we could ever find were sprung traps and a bit of blood and fur. I told Josephine that I would set a trap for the robbers. So on a cold spring morning I was off. I followed the cougar trail that I showed you and found where the tracks went under some windfall alders.

I set my big leg-hold trap under these downed trees and covered it with snow and branches. I crawled out, looked back at the windfall and figured that there would be no chance to catch anything until my scent had been covered by another fall of snow. I walked back out to the trapline and had gone about 50 yards when behind me came shrieks and yowls fit to make what little hair I have stand straight up. I ran back to the windfall, taking the safety off my gun as I went, got on my knees in the snow with my gun in front and crawled under the downed trees. I could see the cougar was caught by a hind leg. It was cowering back, snarling, and trying to get out the other side. The mountain lion gave a loud scream and leaped for me. The chain on the trap snapped. I started firing. The cougar landed on me and knocked me backwards with my knees twisted under me. I don't remember how many times I had fired. I just lay there, imagining the mess I was in. The cougar didn't move. I pushed him off and untangled myself. The cougar was dead. I checked myself over. I was covered in blood, but as it turned out all of it belonged to the cougar.

My heavy winter clothes and boots had done their job. I sat down and waited for my heart to slow down."

We were amazed at the story, but Bert did one better. He gave the cougar skin to us, saying that it was so full of holes that no one would want it. I counted the bullet holes in the skin. There are six.

Since 1956 to the present, that cougar skin has covered our piano bench. It is a little worse for wear as we have had 4 german shepherds over the years and everyone of them has nibbled on it.

Shortly after, Bert died of a heart attack.

In the spring of 1957 Dad and another fisheries inspector, Harry Grainger, were doing a patrol on the Dean River which empties into Kimsquit Channel. On the bank of the river is an old Indian cemetery. They both noticed a freshly painted grave house. This was unusual as no one was buried that way anymore. Bert Robson's name was painted on the door.

That spring I started working on the "booming grounds". This was on the tide flats in the Bella Coola Inlet and was where logs were placed in "booms" to be transported by tug boats to sawmills in the Vancouver area. Our foreman was a big Bella Coola Norwegian, "Pinky" Christensen. Work involved sorting the logs and arranging them into "flat rafts" that could be towed to New Westminister. To hold the boom together each log had a spike driven into it which was attached to a cable by metal loops called "dogs". This process involved wearing cork boots, that is boots with spikes in the bottom so one could walk on floating logs. Tools were pike poles, sledge hammers, for driving the spikes, and wrenches for the cables and of course, boom chains. For the first month falling off a log happened to me every day.

Our work on a boom began at high tide by putting the logs in position. At low tide the actual work was done of pulling cables and pounding in spikes. Of course some times a high tide occurred in the dark. Most loggers did not like this work because of the nights spent on the water. No one wore life jackets back then.

Pounding those big spikes into the logs was a lot of work. Pinky gave me a fourteen pound hammer at first. This was so most of the pounding was done with gravity helping on the down swing so spikes did get into the wood. Of course lifting the hammer in the air was tiring work. Towards the end of my first year at this I was using an eight pound hammer.

After a cold winter a warm spring arrived. Mom started talking about going to Fraser Lake. This expedition was decided on because the road out to Williams Lake was actually completed. In June, I said goodbye to Pinky Christensen and picked up my last cheque. We packed the car, filled up the gas tank and Mom, Brian and I were off over the "hill".

Many stories have been written about this "hill". For those who haven't heard of the way out of Bella Coola I will put in my little history. Apparently the first Norwegian settlers had been promised a road out to civilization. The government was very slow to act. A road was built to Anahim Lake from Williams Lake. Then nothing for years. No amount of letter writing to the government did any good. A citizen's group was formed, led by Leslie Kopas' dad, Cliff. All previous surveys showed a road to be too expensive. Another way was proposed to come in down mud and gravel hills. A road could be built in this location for far less money. Two cat groups started. One was from Anahim Lake and one from Bella Coola. These cats met in 1953. Finally in 1956 a passable road was completed.

Well now we can start on our journey. Mom was in the front seat of the 49 Plymouth. Brian was in the back. We reached the hill and started up. The roadway was very rough and dusty. Rocks were bouncing down on us from above which meant that another car was above us on a switch back. Our engine heated up. There was nothing to do but hope that our engine didn't quit.

We finally reached a level spot and stopped and talked with another car for awhile. Apparently we weren't all the way up. Still more hill to climb. On reaching the top mom started singing a song. "We rode the old hill. We got to the top. Now we're going to Anahim to see the Chinaman!"

On Second Switchback- 1956

This seems like a good place for a little story about the hill.

It seems a Bella Coola family was traveling out for the first time, Mom, Dad, Grandma and a young boy and girl.

"Daddy, I have to go to the bathroom." Car stops and the girl does what she has to do. The car starts again.

"Daddy, Daddy, I have to go to the bathroom too." Car stops and the boy does what he has to do. The car is on its way again.

"Daddy, I don't feel good. I'm going to be sick".... By this time Daddy is losing his patience. The car is on its way again and this time is climbing the hill.

"Daddy, I don't feel good"

Dad stops the car and angrily yells, "Listen kids that's enough!" I don't want to hear anything until we get to the top! This is a dangerous climb! Understand! No nothing! NO STOPPING!"

The car was bouncing badly over the rough rocks. The engine radiator was boiling over!

"Daddy! Daddy! Daddy!"

"No nothing!" hollers Dad.

Finally the car gets to the top. "Now! What is it?"

"Grandma fell out!"

The above story was told to me by Larry Levelton.

On with our story. We passed Anahim Lake without any trouble. Ten miles later a tire went "POP". Ohoh, a flat tire. This was changed and we were on our way again.

The country flattened out. The road was a dusty single track. There were more open spaces. Cows could be seen along the road. There weren't many trees. Ten miles later another "BAM flopflopflop!" Another tire! This time it was a blowout. We only had one spare. Now we had two flats. So much for my plans. I had forgotten a tire repair kit and pump. There was nothing now to do but wait for help. Two and a half hours later an oil truck came along. One of our flats got tied to its top. The driver told us that there was a garage about twenty miles ahead. Leaving Mom and Brian with the car beside an old cabin I climbed in the oil truck and was off.

"Here is the garage. I'll help you get the tire off. Good Luck." and he left me standing in front of an old service station. I rolled the tire over to the rust covered gas pumps and found that the whole place was closed. In fact it had been closed for years.

Now what? I looked around and found a pair of cowboys in the back at an old kitchen table playing crib and drinking coffee. I told them of my predicament. "No problem. I have tire irons, pump and patches in my pickup. I am on my way home. It's only twenty miles off the road.

When we get there you can fix the tire. I'll have supper then we can go find your car and your mom." By the time we arrived at his house it was getting dark and cold too. The cowboy, I will call "Stretch" brought out a gas lantern. I fixed the tire while he had supper. We left and returned to the old Plymouth. Mom and Brian were sure glad to see us. He helped change the tire and offered mom a drink from a pocket flask. "I'll be on my way now." He walked over to the small log cabin. Beside it was a stable, which contained a horse. He told us that he was employed by a local ranch and would get an early start on his fencing chores. "You could sleep in the cabin if you have blankets. Warmer than the car."

Saddling his horse Stretch rode off into the dark.

The blankets were fetched from the car. We made ourselves as comfortable as we could. Head clearance in these cabins was five or six feet and no windows. The door was a piece of old cow skin. Packrats again! In fact packrats filled the place. Our blankets were taken back to the car.

We did get to Fraser Lake within a day. Other mishaps occurred but nothing serious.

After a month we were on our way back. Grandma had decided to come too. I did run into a car on a narrow bridge and dented a fender. But I was saving the real trouble for the hill.

Our car had some rusted out spots in the floor boards. Since the summer had been dry and hot, dust was coming up through the cracks and covering everything inside. We reached the top of the "hill."

"Well, we won't have to worry about overheating on the way down."

The road down was dusty and very rough. I was in second deciding to gear down when boulders started coming down on the road in front of us. I put on the brakes to slow down. By this time there was nothing much left of them but a bad smell. We hit the boulders. The car bounded almost off the road. Bang Crash! The gearshift lever jumped into neutral. I couldn't get it back into gear. I pushed harder on the brakes and got the transmission into high gear which was better than nothing. There was only one more corner. We made it and slowly stopped. From the back Grandma was laughing. So was Brian. I turned around and could hardly see them for all the dust. Grandma and Brian were brown all over. We sat there and laughed. Tears were running down grandma's face leaving brown trails. At least we didn't lose her coming down the hill.

Now school was starting. By the time spring arrived only Daryl and I were left in grade twelve. The girls all got married. The boys all left for work. I was on University Program and so had plans. Daryl had plans too. He wanted to take courses in Diesel Mechanics and continue in the forest industry.

He eventually owned a logging truck and got tired of that. He started flying and finally was the owner of a large airline on the coast.

With the beginning of school a new boy with a young sister arrived. This was Gunde Frostrup. He came in with family from the lower mainland. Gunde taught us a lot of things. He had all Elvis Presley's records and played his guitar all the time. It is a good thing our school principal was an easygoing man. Gunde sure brightened up our school.

Gunde playing guitar. Me, with case playing small mouth organ

This was a happy time. There were no big worries.. The above photograph represents this time in our lives. The valley sheltered our lives like the Shire in the "Hobbit."

I mentioned earlier that all music in the valley was "home grown" Gunde played his guitar. I played the piano. Daryl played the guitar. Between us we actually played well enough so that people would dance to our music.

During our final sports day. I was finally beaten in a 100 yard race by Ernie Sollid. This must have impressed him because he eventually followed me and became a phys ed teacher too.

Spring came and Dad was promoted again. He did ask me if it was all right because I was in grade twelve. I told him to go ahead with the promotion and another move.

I do now believe that Mom and Dad led a life where they just had to keep moving. Each time they had to "up root" was a time of excitement and expectation.

When I did get married and built a house I told my wife, Coral, that we would stay in one place forever.

Chapter Twelve

QUEEN CHARLOTTE ISLANDS. MASSET HIGH

Here we are, packing again. The government paid for the move. Everything was put in crates and placed on the Bella Coola dock to await the Union steamship, the Catala. The date was May 13th. Strange because that was the date, May 13th, when we arrived here four years before. We made the trip to Ocean Falls. This wasn't such a big deal this time because of all the time spent on the Fisheries boats. All our furniture was unloaded and we waited for the boat to the Charlottes. We had a piano this time and a big black cat. Even my old car, the 49 Plymouth, came with us.

Ocean Falls was a bit nicer this time with sunny days but was still very windy in the afternoons. Dad, Brian and I were down on the docks again. This time we were watching a large aircraft approaching. It was a twin engined Canso, This aircraft made a wide roaring turn and landed in front of us, bouncing into the large waves.

Dad said, "That's got to be Sheldon Luck, No one can fly like him."

When the plane docked, Sheldon got out, handshakes all round, Dad introduced me to him.

Sheldon grinned and said, "So this is the little guy all grown up!" I got a bit red with this.

Later Mom told me what that was all about. In the winter before I was born, mom, who was a quite small lady, was having trouble when she was pregnant with me. A mercy flight had been arranged to fly her and another girl with appendicits out of Fort Nelson to the hospital in Prince George.

This was late spring. All was covered with snow. Sheldon was the pilot. The engine started coughing. Sheldon muttered, "Oh oh", and some other proper words for the occasion. The motor finally quit for good and Sheldon made a landing on the frozen Peace River. They were rescued the next day after spending a cold cold night in a small old trappers cabin which was loaded with, you guessed it, Pack Rats!

A Canso like Sheldon's

Back to Ocean Falls. Sheldon left with one of his famous take offs This was by opening the throttle wide on one engine, causing the plane to do a quick circle. Closing down that engine he opened the other engine all the way to do a full turn in the other direction. Then he applied full power to the first engine. This creates a figure eight and the aircraft is on plane and in the air without much take-off room. At one time Sheldon Luck was the head pilot for Canadian Pacific Airlines. A book has been written about him, "Walking on Air".

After three days we were loaded and on our way again. We had an afternoon stop in Kitimat, which was a new city at this time. An over night stay in

Prince Rupert was necessary as well. We had cabins aboard the boat.

Early in the morning we left for Masset from Rupert. Masset was the village on the Queen Charlotte Islands that we would be living in. This was a nine hour crossing if the weather was good.

Everyone enjoyed the trip except our cat, Curly, who thought he was going to die from sea sickness. One of the younger crew members had taken the cat from his cage in the hold to his quarters at the forward part of the boat. The swell from the open sea caused the front of the boat to travel 20 feet up and down. On the 20 feet up Curly held on to the steel deck with his claws and made faces. On the 20 feet down he puked.

We were traveling west into the open ocean in a bright clear morning. No land was in sight. The water changed from a coast dark green to a pacific blue. We definitely were going to a new land. After we reached the islands the ship traveled west along an enormous long beach. Everything was flat. Arriving at the seaside town of Masset the ship tied to an identical dock to the one in Bella Coola. This dock seemed much bigger because there were no mountains pressing down upon it.

We disembarked and met a friend of Dad's from the Fisheries. My family, Mom and Dad, brother Brian and I walked off the dock, past the local cannery and down a sandy street to our new home. I was shocked to see that it was the same as our house in Bella Coola, same white, same green trim, same white picket fence, same lawn, and same clothes line off the back porch. Inside all was the same as well. To be different Brian and I switched bedrooms. He got the right and I got the left.

The next day we walked to school, which was only a short distance from our house. I met the principal who was my teacher. He introduced me to the grade twelve class. Here I was, "new kid in town" again. This class was composed of four natives, the cannery manager's daughter and myself. This felt strange to me to be in a minority group. I found out that the Indians here actually treated us whites better than us whites treated the Indians in the rest of B.C.

One boy, Dick Bellis, quickly became my friend. The first weekend a group of us went out to the North Beach. This was a long sand and gravel beach that went on forever. When the tide was out, there was a couple of hundred yards of sand. Beyond the high tide line was another 50 yards of fine sand and driftwood. The day was sunny and warm. The sand was hot. We scared up a large herd of deer that had come down to do some grazing. We went out to a rocky point of land, called Naikun (nyecoon) Dick found some rock cod eggs. We ate them. They crunched in your mouth and the insides tasted a bit fishy.

The principal, Mr. Wright, had a good way to teach the grade eleven and twelves. He enrolled each student in correspondence courses necessary to complete the grade. He supervised each student and helped where necessary. At the end of the school day, the grade twelves went out for a coffee and a smoke, came back about four o'clock and then finished the day at six. Faith Simpson the cannery managers daughter and I were on "university program". All the rest were on "general program". Dick had already made up his mind to go down south the following year to take a heavy duty mechanics course. This he did and came back to work in the logging industry fixing trucks. When he finally retired he was in charge of truck maintenance and repairs for Macmillan and Blodel, Queen Charlotte Division. "Mac and Blo" was the largest forestry company in BC at that time.

The school year ending on grad day in June went very fast. This was the largest grad class that Masset ever had, Six of us, Doug Hageman, Merle Davidson, Dick Bellis, Lily Bennet, Faith Simpson and me.

After grad I was on the way out to Fraser Lake. Transportation was on a small Fisheries Vessel, the Nichola Post. This took me to Prince Rupert. We left at daybreak from Masset. Aboard, besides me were the cook and skipper. This turned out to be an eventful trip. The Nichola couldn't make it out past Rose Spit because of wind and huge waves blowing from the south. When the boat finally started to across the sea was so rough that the skipper called a May Day. I didn't know this because I was too busy hanging on in the galley. This is the kitchen on the boat to you land lubbers. Most all the dishes jumped out of their racks, cupboards were emptied of their contents as well as my stomach.

The next day saw me on the passenger train to Fraser Lake. I was now 17 and couldn't wait to get to work. I was to drive truck with cousin Larry.

The summer of 1957 turned out to be one of rain and more rain. This was not the kind of weather for driving trucks on dirt bush roads. The only breaks we got from the rain and the mud were the frequent thunder storms. Besides learning to drive trucks we mastered other skills as well. Such as: putting chains on after you had gotten stuck. repiling your load after your truck had gotten stuck, and how to drive so you didn't get stuck. These trucks, L170 Internationals, were old and worn out. Larry's was called Red, and mine was called Green. If everything worked out, 4 loads of rough lumber could be taken from the bush camps to the planer mill in a day. That is if nothing broke. Five dollars was given to us for every load that made it to the planer mill. Larry and I worked most nights to repair and service the beasts.

Our furthest haul was from Boral Lake. To get there the trucks had to travel up a three mile grade. At the top of the hill when returning, the trucks always had to stop for a "brake check".

This I was doing. The pedal was pushed. It went straight to the floor. Oh oh, no brakes… The engine died at the same time. The truck with its heavy load of lumber was still moving over the crest of the hill. The brakes wouldn't work. The engine wouldn't start. The truck was creaking and rumbling, more speed, faster and faster. A turn was coming! I made this one. Speed was now greater. Trying to make the next corner, the front wheel went off the road on the down side. I missed a large tree by inches. Wham! This tree made contact with the bull board between the cab and the load. The truck slammed to a stop. All that could be seen out the front window was sky and far away mountains. A large rock could be heard crashing down and down the mountain side. I sat until my shaking stopped. Soon Larry came by and he got out and hummed and hawed. Later that day we came back with Red, empty. Red was loaded with the lumber from Green. Red was used to tow Green back on the road. The brakes were repaired and Green made it back to town. This turned out to be Green's last haul.

Next week I was not a truck driver but was now a lumber piler at a mill on Francois Lake called "East End". Here my time was spent piling lumber produced by the mill into truckloads for Larry and

Jimmy. I did talk to the various crewmembers and was quite fascinated by the saws called the "Edger".

At the end of this summer I got a ride to Vancouver with the company accountant. This was to enroll in my final place of learning. This was the University of British Columbia. Let's see if I haven't forgotten a school:

> Correspondence
> Fraser Lake
> Fraser Lake North
> Vanderhoof
> South Park
> Lonsdale
> Dashwood
> Qualicum High
> Alpha Junior High
> Booth Memorial High
> Sir Alexander Mackenzie
> Masset Elementary Secondary
> University of British Columbia

On all our family moves a return to familiar Fraser Lake was a blessing.

Chapter Thirteen

UBC 1957

The accountant let me off in Vancouver on the corner of Georgia and Granville. I had with me a duffel bag full of clothes I was down in Vancouver a week before classes started. This should be a good time to turn myself back into a city boy.

I was wearing jeans, and a buckskin jacket with fringe down each arm and across the back. This was dressup clothes in Fraser Lake and the Charlottes.

I checked myself into the Ambassador Hotel. Here I stayed for two days, going to movies and shopping for clothes for school. The screech of brakes and sirens from fire trucks and police cars kept me awake most nights.

Oh, I didn't say so, but before I left Bella Coola, the principal of the school there had helped me enroll in UBC on a first year program. I also had a place to stay at Acadia Camp that was right at

UBC. My mom helped me pack a brand new trunk with stuff I would need. Again, the principal, Mr. Loosmore, helped me by telling me what I should take with me. This trunk was pretty heavy. Contents included, a typewriter, a radio, a reading lamp, an electric iron, extra bedding, and extra clothes. The clothes were good and practical for the north. This included: mackinaw jackets, jeans, and Prince Rupert rain gear.

This trunk was to be sent by Union Steamship and would be waiting for me when arriving at UBC

Well now was the time to tackle University. I dressed in all my northern splendour, jeans, snap button western shirt and my buckskin jacket. I got on the trolley bus for the University. This took me to the "Gates". From here I transferred to a local bus that took me in to this wonderful looking park next to the Book Store on campus. There were lots of students here. Most looked like they knew where they were going. Most were packing armloads of books. There were a few gawking around like me. I soon found a map of how to get to Acadia Camp. This was about a mile away. When I arrived I found a line to stand in. An hour later I was given some sheets, blankets, a meal pass, a key and a dorm and room number.

NEW KID IN TOWN

This was temporary accommodation in another camp called, "Youth Training Camp" or "YTC".

All us northerners were placed at "YTC". These accommodations were "dignified" with the name "huts". Acadia, Youth Training Camp and Fort Camp were left over from the return of the veterans after WWII. Later us northerners were moved down to Acadia Camp.

That first day was spent getting to know some of the new students. It wasn't so bad this time because there were so many "new kids in town." One was Jack Collier from Terrace. The place where we were to eat was back at Acadia. So back we went for lunch and stood in line for half an hour. After we ate, Jack and I walked back to the Campus to find the Registration Building where we stood in line again. This line was to pay our Tuition Fees. When this was done, we were told to go stand in that line, to enroll in the first year classes and get our room and instructor assignments. A list of the books used in that class were given out. Now a trip to the book exchange was necessary and another line to stand in. All our books had to be paid for. Second hand books were available. At the end of the year one could sell the books back.

A big joke at this time was to get freshmen, that was Jack and me, to stand in the wrong line. "Oh, you are in the wrong line. This one is for second year students!" "Oh, you are in the wrong line. This one is to apply for bursaries!" "Oh, you are in the wrong line. This one is for off campus accommodation!"

On the way back to Acadia Camp with our arms full of books an older student wearing a red sweater stopped us. "Hey! You! What are you doing out of uniform. The next time I see you be properly dressed or into the pond you go!"

Arriving back at YTC it was found out that the first week was "Frosh Orientation Week!" Hazing was not only allowed but encouraged. To escape punishment one had to be suitably attired and treat older students with "respect". This meant wearing pajamas and a special frosh beany (hat) to all classes and be willing at all times to do chores for the senior classmen. Jack actually wore his pajamas the first day.

I decided not to. I did get thrown into the Library pond a few times. I even managed to throw an engineer in. Actually we both went in together.

This is from the UBC Annual

After a month, I put all my Northern Clothes in my trunk and cut off all the fringe from my buckskin jacket. I was now wearing proper preppy clothes. I was even wearing a skinny tie to classes. What would the Bella Coola kids think of me now?

The year continued with lots of struggles, especially in English, Physics, French and Psychology. My final grade for English was twenty-six percent. Low marks in English were usually given to those of us with an environmental disadvantage. Very few from the North country made it to university. I was the first one on both sides of our family to take education this far. My mom was born in Sweden as well as many of my relatives. "Vee spoke fawny". I did most of my high schooling in the north. In Bella Coola the entire town spoke "vit a norveejun accent".

The rest of UBC 1958-1962

During the next years my marks steadily improved. I switched from "Engineering" to "Physical Education and Recreation". Gymnastics became my sport of choice and I was on the varsity gym team for the entire time spent at UBC. This kept me out of trouble with all the time spent practicing and going to gym meets. Our team competed in the Northwest Collegiate circle. The teams included, Washington State, University of Washington, Eastern Washington, Central Washington, Western Washington and Pacific Lutheran College. Our furthest regular travel was to Washington State which was in a small college town, Pullman, just east of Spokane. We also competed in the Provincials in BC and Alberta. Most Thursday afternoons found us putting on gym shows at the major high schools in Vancouver.

During my last two years I was running the University Area gym classes for young boys, As part of our training we had to teach the first year students sports. The Physical Education students were paid for this. We got $1.40 per class. This kept me supplied with coffee and donuts.

This pic appeared in the
Vancouver Sun newspaper
Bill Cunningham, Photographer

After winning the Pacific North West title
I'm in the middle in the back row

I only spent one year at Acadia Camp as I found that life in the camp made study rather difficult. Each year a move was made further away from the Campus. My last year was almost downtown Vancouver. Life was good. I graduated with a Bachelor of Physical Education in the Spring of 1962. I was on the Varsity Gymnastics Team for all the time at UBC and was awarded three "Big Block" sweaters.

Classes were classes and not too interesting.

Again, as in my previous schooling, the good stuff occurred in the summer.

Chapter Fourteen

THE UNIVERSITY SUMMERS

SUMMER 1958

The summers always started with "getting home". The first time was a trip from Vancouver to the Charlottes. This started with a dash from Vancouver to Terrace. There were four in the car, a 1952 Ford hotrod. Each of us took turns driving. We did this 850 miles in 16 hours, averaging over 50 miles per hour. Only half the distance was paved.

After a short sleep at Jack Colllier's, I was hitching a ride to Rupert. At a gas station a ride was found This was in an old Model A convertible with "Century Sam". 1958 being BC's centennial year, Century Sam, real name, Sid Williams, had been hired by the government to help with the Centennial Celebrations. Century Sam was a prospector and stopped whenever he saw a rock. The distance to Prince Rupert was 90 miles and took us 10 hours.

In Rupert after checking in to the Prince Rupert Hotel I went down to the docks to find a ride over to the Charlottes.

This turned out to be a Seine Boat heading to Langara Island. The boat was leaving at 4 AM. After a short sleep I was on the boat. Ten hours later another boat was found heading to Masset

The first part of the summer was spent on a public works road crew, which was building the first road from Masset to Port Clements.

This road would head south and us, the "dry town" of Masset would be connected with the "wet town" of Queen Charlotte City. There was a beer parlor in Port Clements and further to the south a government liquor store in Queen Charlotte City. This did give the road crew a great reason to work quickly.

My job was to work with our cat driver, Clarence and his old TD14. This caterpillar tractor Clarence named "Violet".

Finally the day arrived, our foreman, Arden, said, "Well boys. This is the day!" Arden started off over the last 100 yards of rough gravel in his old pickup. He bounced to a stop 30 feet from the bridge which was being built by the Port Clements crew.

Our crew of seven managed to make a road with planks torn from the new bridge deck and got Arden on his way.

Arden showed up later in the afternoon. He was very very "happy". The crew had backfilled the last holes, packed the gravel and repaired the damage to the bridge. Everyone got in two gravel trucks and Arden's pickup and headed down to celebrate the unofficial opening of the road to Queen Charlotte City. That is everyone but me. I was only 18. Darn! I was given the job of taking the third gravel truck back to Masset and telling the good/bad news to the wives of the crew.

The next day I drove the truck back to the bridge. The crew slowly started working. They were not in very good shape having been up all night with their friends, Wobbly Pop and Captain Morgan.

Arden went to Masset to report. The three gravel trucks had their drivers back. The loader at the gravel pit was working. Clarence was on his cat and I was doing my usual with a shovel.

"Gee, George is driving rather fast." I said to myself. George, who was putting top dressing on the road roared by in his gravel truck and waved with a silly grin. The next load was even faster.

Arden came back from town, "Gawd Dammit! The big boss from Rupert is on his way over to inspect our road!"

George roared by in a cloud of dust, grinning and waving at Arden. "What the hell is wrong with him?"

"Oh." Arden got George to stop, took him and a case of beer out of the truck cab and put them both behind a stump.

"Now George, you STAY!!! Monte, you drive the truck!"

The big boss arrived and was very pleased with what he saw. He shook all our hands and left. All that is except for George who was taking a nap. My promotion to truck driver only lasted to the next day. George was "well" again.

I was laid off soon after because the road was finished.

After this I was working for Walt Perlstrom, a local man who did just about anything that needed to be done in the town. His crew were the high school boys, Doug, Dick, Johnny, and now me. We hauled firewood, gravel and trash, cleared underbrush and cut firewood. We were also the town fire department.

One day Dick and I went down to the beach where two families were building a couple of seine boats. We helped out a bit by using draw planes on the hull planking. Walt heard us talking about the boats. He went over to them and soon had cooked up another way to make money. He promised the boat families that he could cut boards for them with the old Masset sawmill. This mill had shut down at the end of the War. That was thirteen years before. The mill had been used to cut spruce for the Mosquito bombers.

Walt was soon looking at the old equipment. "Well, I'm pretty sure we can get it goin' again."

We were soon busy. Walt tinkered with the old White Diesel. This engine was six feet tall and eight feet long. Soon the White was running. We repaired all the old drive belts, which went from the main shaft to various parts of the mill. All the pulleys were cleaned and greased. The drive clutches were repaired.

Walt slowly released the clutch on the main shaft. Wheels started turning, slowly at first, then faster and faster. The whole building was shaking. When the main shaft got up to speed the shaking turned into a steady vibration. Everything was working!

The engine was shut down. Then the mills components were put into proper order. This meant a lot of grease. All moving parts were checked. Walt looked after the headsaw. Dick's job was the carriage and tracks. Johnny, Dick's younger brother, was in charge of the jack ladder and winches to get the logs into the mill. I got the edger in shape. Doug looked after the cross cut saw and slab chain which took the waste wood out to a large pile.

I was given the job of looking after the edger because the year before when not driving truck I was working in a sawmill and had actually seen an edger. The main task was to sharpen all seven of the circular saws that cut the slabs from the head saw into boards of the proper width.

The boat families, Edenshaw and White, found large cedars, both red and yellow. These were felled into the inlet or close to water. They were then dragged into the water with their fish boats and floated to the mill. These trees were perfect.

Soon the sawmill operation began. Johnny took the logs from the water, up the jack ladder, and we all helped to roll them on to the log carriage. Arden. the sawyer, started cutting slabs of bark from the large logs. This log was almost "squared" into one huge timber. The waste wood went straight through the mill to Doug who sent this scrap onto the conveyor chain and out to the slab pile.

After the bark slabs were taken off four sides the real work could begin. Walt put this big timber through the circular headsaws and produced large planks. These were either one or two inches in thickness. Dick, now the tail sawyer, with my help put the first large plank on the edger table. This plank went through the edger saws. It was my job to move the blades to get dimensional lumber. From a piece one inch thick and three feet wide the edger could make two one by eights and three one by fives. The boat owners wanted most of the wood as one by fives. After going through the edger the finished lumber was stacked by Doug

This process only worked for a little while because Doug would get behind. He was trying to do the work of four men. We would have to shut the head saw down and go help him.

The mill stopped every once in awhile for breakdowns, or no logs. When this happened we would cut the slab wood into stove lengths, fill up a truck and deliver it. I guess every house in town got a load or two of our wood.

Finally the orders for boat lumber were completed and we were back to our regular work. At this time Richfield Oil showed up on the island to put in some "Wild Cat Wells". They were just exploring to see what was under the island. Arden and his crew were immediately hired to improve the roads along North Beach where an oil well was to be drilled.

One day I was dumping loads of gravel into a swamp with a gravel truck. I got the truck stuck. We were using another truck to pull us out. Hooking up my truck to the tow truck I slipped and ended up to my waist in water. Arden showed up and says. "Job's over boys. We have to get out of the bush. Fire Season!" This did not make sense to us because when working alongside North Beach in a swamp one couldn't even light a cigarette, too wet!

Soon though, Arden had us working unloading a freighter. This was filled with sacks and sacks of stuff that the oil men called "mud". This lasted for about a week. After that I was given another job of driving a new pickup truck for Richfield's manager. I also had to go for this and that.

This "gopher" job lasted until my grandfather Engelson died, late September. Dad and I took a plane down to Victoria for the funeral. After that it was time for UBC.

SUMMER 1959

During the spring of 1959 Dad received a posting to the town of Smithers. This is halfway between Prince Rupert and Prince George.

In early May I found my way to Smithers this time in a little Austin. For summer work this year I was employed first by the Fisheries to repair winter damage to a station on Babine Lake. This was nothing but a fishing holiday.

Later I joined a survey crew for the Fisheries in a town called Hazelton This was 50 miles away from Smithers.

Hagwilget Canyon where we
worked for the summer
Bridge is 250 ft off water.

We, Roger Kearns, Jerry Pratt and I, were to find out how successful a fisheries winter project had been. An obstruction had been blasted from the Canyon on the Bulkley River.

Our survey showed that the blasting had been a success. The rapids and falls had been completely eliminated. The bears couldn't catch salmon. The eagles couldn't catch salmon. We couldn't catch salmon…

In the canyon, Hagwilget, where the rocks used to be, we fished with hook and line, drift seines and dip nets. Rodger even put on a skin diving suit to check for fish… Nothing…

The native people couldn't catch salmon… oops.

We watched from the shore as two older Indians came down to the river each day and set nets. They returned the next day and the next and the next. The woman shook her head. There never was a fish caught. The Indians, that is the young bucks after trips to the beer parlor, took their frustrations out on us. Rocks were thrown from the bridge. A bottle dropped and exploded beside me, Challenges for fights with us were given.

One night there was a pounding on our door and yelling from outside, "Open up you white man! Come out and fight!" Jerry and I were pretty scared. The big Indian, who we called "Skull", was beating on the door. Skull had an eye poked out and walked around without an eye patch. You wouldn't wanta to show him to little children

Roger slipped his jeans on and said to himself, "One Two Three!" and slammed open the door.

Skull was knocked off the low porch. Roger landed on him and pushed the back of a comb against his throat.

Skull yelled, "Kill me white man!" a long pause, "Coward!"

Roger talked low to him for awhile and taking the "knife" off his throat promised Skull he wouldn't kill him.

We don't know how Roger did it, but Skull was friendly with us after that.

The next evening Roger Kearns went to an Indian Council meeting. He was quite a diplomat and managed to keep the hair on our heads by talking with the elders, promising that everything would be right. The government would make everything right. Little did Roger know what his words would foretell or how long it would take to make "everything right".

Well, a long time time passed. In April 2009, my phone rang.

A girl was on the other end, "Are you Harold Engelson?"

"That was my fathers name. I sometimes use the name as well."

"Where can I find your father?"

"He passed away."

"Oh, I'm trying to find someone who worked for the fisheries in Hazelton in 1959." *This was fifty years ago!*

"Oh, I did." I said.

I was told that the Indians were suing the Federal Government for loss of their native fisheries. After a few more questions back and forth, I found that I was the last one alive that had worked on that project. I told this lawyer what had happened at that time.

"Would you be willing to appear as a witness for the defendants in the case, that is the Department of Indian Affairs? The trial will start at the end of April."

I told the lawyer, no. I wouldn't be a very good witness because I was on the side of the natives. The lawyer thanked me for my time.

The following was taken from a newspaper:

ALFRED JOSEPH et al v. HER MAJESTY THE QUEEN as represented by THE MINISTER OF INDIAN AFFAIRS AND NORTHERN DEVELOPMENT"

Vancouver, British Columbia – (April 28, 2009) – A small First Nation community in northern BC has made history for itself today. On the eve of a precedent-setting trial Canada agreed to compensate the people of Hagwilget Village near Hazelton for the complete destruction of their fishery by Canada fifty years ago. The trial was scheduled to start this morning, but on Friday afternoon Canada agreed to a judgment for $21.5 million dollars to compensate the Hagwilget people for not having fish for fifty years and for the damages to their culture as a result of the devastation of their fishery.

Hagwilget Chief Dora Wilson stated after a community meeting on Sunday, April 26th, "Our members have overwhelmingly supported the decision of the elected Chief and Council to settle our case for $21.5 million. This award will be established in a trust to advance the education in our languages, our culture and the future of Hagwilget."

In the winter of 1959 representatives from Department of Fisheries dynamited several large boulders in the Bulkley River next to the reserve, completely destroying that First Nation's active fishery there. The Hagwilget people say that the blasting was done in complete disregard of the Hagwilget people's rights to their fishery and was aimed to provide more salmon for the commercial canneries. The Hagwilget fishery had been used by the Gitxsan and Wet'suwet'en continuously since before contact. It was one of the richest Aboriginal fisheries on the Skeena River system which include the Bulkley River.

Chief Wilson tells of how in 1959 a group of women tried to throw rocks on the men dynamiting the fishery. "They knew what we were about to lose and they tried to do everything in their power to stop it." As she explains, "From being one of the richest and proudest communities in the Northwest, respected by our neighbours and those farther away, we became beggars asking for fish from others if they had any to spare."

The Hagwilget people have seen the downward spiral that has resulted from the loss of identity. Many believe they can link substance abuse and suicide attempts at Hagwilget to the loss of the fishery.

"We didn't lose just the fish and the value they gave us, but also a sense of who we were," says Chief Wilson. "That fishery was the main thing binding us together and also the time when we conveyed elements of our culture and language to our young people. It happened in our smokehouses where we prepared the fish, on the trails to and from the canyon, during the fishing, in our homes and in the village each fishing season. With the fishery gone, it all just kind of unraveled."

Well, now to get back to the past. At the end of the summer. the three of us drove back down to UBC. I started my third year, Jerry, his fourth and Roger was just beginning graduate studies.

SUMMER 1960

Summer again. My "home" was still Smithers. The ride home this time was by car. I had been staying with Mike Hoskins who was from Smithers. His dad owned the Ford Agency in town. We would drive new cars from Vancouver to Hoskins's Ford Agency.

Since I was getting a bit older, 20 now, I got a job with a bit more responsibility. This was to be a patrolman on the Kitimat River, This patrolman was to observe and make reports on the fish and fishermen in the Kitimat River System. His duties also were to keep and maintain trails along the river and its tributaries.

The family car was to be my transportation. Dad again had a government vehicle. A place to stay was arranged in a cabin on Lakelse Lake.

When I got to the cabin I found that it didn't even have electricity. This was going to be fun! I spent most of my time walking up and down all the tributaries of the river. The main part could be got to by car. However all the tributaries on the north side of the river could only be seen by hiking or riding with a section crew on the railroad. I got to know the foreman quite well. He was tall, well mannered and could speak English. His crew was all Portuguese and couldn't speak any English. The highway was on the south side and the railway was on the north. I sent in weekly reports, giving my time spent on the job and what I was done each day. After two weeks a letter of reprimand arrived.

"Dear Mr. Engelson, Please show that you have worked only 40 hours per week and take two days off as well."

What was I to do? Soon I found a great way to pass the time. I got a second job at Lakelse Hotspring Resort as a lifeguard. I worked in the evening and ten or twelve hours each Saturday and Sunday. This fit in pretty good as at UBC I was taking a lot of sports which included hours and hours of swimming instruction. So besides "life guarding" I taught swimming and was the resort's First Aid man.

During the time at the Hotsprings I met another boy, Ron. I asked him to go with me down the Kitimat River in a canoe as part of my river inspections. A canoe was requisitioned and when it arrived we took a couple of trips before setting out in the river. Ron sat in the back with his rifle. I was in the front. Thankfully life jackets were also worn. Away we went on this 20 mile journey. We were dumped while trying to go through our first rapids. We learned a lot with that. We only capsized two more times.

Shooting rapids is lots of fun. Going down one long set the canoe rounding a slight bend and ahead of us smack dab in the middle of our run was a huge brown grizzly bear fishing. His backside was towards us. Ron and I yelled and screamed and beat on the canoe rails with our paddles. The bear was deaf! Ron shouts to me, "Duck your head. I'm going to shoot!" I grabbed on to the canoe with both hands, ducked my head and "Bang!" Ron shot the grizzly in his back-side. That got the bear's attention. It turned and roared at us. We were screaming, yelling and waving our arms. Ron shot his gun in the air. The bear looked at us with wide eyes, stood up, turned and ran straight down the rapids with us on his tail. We caught up to him and managed to pass him. The ride ended with us doing slow circles in a quiet pool. We didn't see the bear again. The trip continued with much less excitement.

Towards the end of August a fisheries inspector arrived and I was to take him out for a couple of days on a river tour. Kitimat was a very high producer in Chum and Spring Salmon. The weather turned absolutely rotten. There was nothing but hard rain.

Early on a Monday morning I picked up Inspector G from a patrol boat at the Kitimat docks. He was dressed in heavy boots, good warm clothes and a heavy Fisheries issue rain coat.

On the way out to our first stream, which would be filled with spawning Chum, I noticed that "G" was constantly taking a nip from a flask. Arriving under the spruce trees by the stream's edge I showed G a favorite deep eddy that was loaded with fish. I also warned G to watch out for "Devil's Club" which was everywhere. The trail went across the pool on a log that was just out of the water. After crossing I turned around and G was gone. His hat was floating. I ran back and saw him looking up at me from under the surface. Reaching down I grabbed the back of his raincoat and got his head out of the water. I dragged him over to a low bank and he managed to crawl out. G sat there with his feet in the water.

An hour later he was back on his patrol boat and in bed. I checked with G the next day to see if he wanted to try another trip. No thank you.

Two days later another inspector arrived. We will call him "P". He asked if I would arrange a trip on the north side of the river with the section crew. The day dawned cold and rainy. In fact the day was worse than when G fell in. This was just the perfect day for my twenty-first birthday, August 31st!

A little explanation is necessary here. The section crew maintained the railway. Their transportation was a small four wheeled vehicle known as a "Speeder" The top speed was 35 miles per hour. One of these little cars could hold six to eight workers sitting sideways back to back. This was what we were to ride on for our journey to the Big Wedeene River.

I introduced Inspector P and Inspector G to the foreman. We climbed on. The bright yellow Speeder slowly built up speed. "Putt Putt PuttPuttPutt…" The rain kept coming down. There was no roof and only a canvas square up forward to keep the wind away. After twenty minutes everyone was soaked through. The speeder was now at maximum speed traveling around a sharp curve with a cliff on the left and the river running fifty feet below on the right.

I looked ahead over the canvas screen.

"Oh No!" Another yellow Speeder appeared coming straight at us! Everything turned into slow motion for me. I could see the heads and wide eyes of the crew on the other car. One jumped off, than another and another. I turned to yell at the two inspectors. They had seen the other train hurtling towards us and had already jumped… They were on the riverside and were tumbling down the steep bank towards the river. The rest of our crewmembers had jumped. I ran off the speeder and managed to keep my feet. At the same time one of our crew ran into a runner coming the other way.

To add to the confusion the Speeder coming towards us had attached to it a 4 wheeled flat car. On it were 6 empty oil drums. WHAM! BANG! BOOM! The two vehicles crashed like two mountain sheep. Both Speeders stood on end before falling over. The oil drums were booming down into the river. Water, oil and gas was everywhere.

Our section foreman grabbed the other foreman and punched him in the head. Each was yelling at each other in Portuguese. Biff! Pow! Bam! The fight went on for awhile. I had sat down on the ground and was laughing until I was crying. What a wonderful birthday present!

G ran up to me, "What is wrong with you! We could have been killed!"

This only made me laugh all the more. When the "smoke" had cleared only two had been hurt. Those were the two crewmen that had run into each other.

A quarter mile away there was a cookhouse for the Iron Mountain Mine. The cook had a radio phone so we got a message back to Kitimat. Another speeder was called out and we went home. Not a bad day.

SUMMER 1961

At the end of this school year a large fisheries vessel, "Laurier", was on its way north from Vancouver to Kitimat. Dad had arranged for me to come home on this. Dad had accepted a new posting and had just transferred from Smithers to Kitimat. This sounded okay. I could stay at home and do the same work as last year. So I thought. There was a problem with this, something called "Nepotism." If I worked in Kitimat, my Dad would be my boss. This was a no no. The fisheries owed me one so I became a "Guardian" at a very isolated spot ten miles from Bella Bella. This was in a small inlet off Spiller Channel called Tinky. The reason for a Guardian at a place like this was that Tinky was a great fishing spot. It was a little bay that connected through to a series of lakes. These were the spawning grounds for a huge amount of Sockeye Salmon. Someone had to be present to stop illegal fishing. A patrol boat would bring food once per week.

I left Kitimat on a large fisheries boat, the Sooke Post, with supplies for the summer.

Arriving at Tinky Bay, all supplies were placed in a work boat, taken to shore and unloaded on the beach. The crew of the Sooke Post said goodbye and left me standing beside the pile of stuff. The tide was low. My first job was to get everything above the high tideline. This included, the bed, tables, chairs and wood stove. There was also a load of tools: axes, hammers, saws, nails, screw drivers, etc. Included was a box of kitchen supplies to get me started. A 16 foot boat and inboard engine was provided as well. This move, above the high tide line, took most of the day. All was covered with a tarp. The bed was packed up to the cabin by nightfall. This cabin was one room, 16 feet by 16. There was a door and one window.

The next day saw the rest of the supplies put away. The hardest job was setting up the stove. This included installing the chimney. Driftwood had to be sawn up and chopped for firewood. Where was the water? No one told me. Rainwater would have to do for now. The water from the roof tasted like oil. During the first week, a trip was made to a creek, which was a quarter mile distant. Two five gallon water containers were filled and brought back.

So, now I could cook, and wash. Another problem surfaced. I went out looking for an outhouse…no outhouse. I did it in the woods.

The fisheries charter vessel, the PML4, Police Motor Launch Number 4, was to come by the next day to pick up my weekly report and take a shopping list to the general store in Shearwater. Shearwater is across the harbour from the Indian village of Bella Bella.

The skipper brought me some grey boat paint for the floor of the cabin and this floor was to be painted in my spare time. My first request was for 28 six foot one by eights to build an outhouse. While waiting for the next weeks delivery the floor was painted, The next week, along with my groceries was a letter asking me why I needed an outhouse and to draw a plan and a proper supply list to construct same. The PML4 waited while I produced this document. This charter vessel arrived next week with my groceries and a shipment of outhouse building material. Two weeks later a Fisheries Inspector arrived to "inspect" the new structure. "Where is the door?" he asked. That was a dumb question as who was going to see me way out here. My nearest neighbour was at Bella Bella.

And so started that summer. Many things were done to keep me from getting too bored. Fishing boats, seiners and gill netters were visited from time to time. Beach combing and exploring kept me busy. I carved a Totem Pole. Dad thought that it was most likely a great example of Indian art by now.

At low tide abalone were plentiful. Fishing was great. Salmon, Cod and Halibut could be caught any time.

My thirteen year old brother Brian hitched a ride on a fisheries plane and stayed with me for two weeks. During this time I had to go to Ocean Falls to write a supplemental exam from UBC. Brian was on his own for two nights. I didn't know at the time that he had never been alone before. When I got back I found that he had not slept at night at all. He sat up each night with a rifle across his knees. During the daytime. He took the boat out and fished all day.

We found the remains of an old Indian village. At the end of the bay was a narrow channel, in some places only ten feet wide. This was a half mile long and opened into a lagoon about one hundred yards across. Tidal water would run in and fill this little lake. When the tide dropped the water would run out leaving a mud expanse. This flat bottom was covered with the remains of stone walls to trap fish.

One Indian gillnetter said, "Tinky used to be the best summer camp. The fisheries stopped us from fishing here years ago and broke down all our rock traps."

The native continued, "In late August the salmon will come in and fill the lagoon. You will be able to walk across the creek on their backs." This last statement I didn't really believe.

The picture of me is with my first halibut. If you can see my left hand you will notice bandages on two fingers. These were cut by the line when the fish took off for the last time. We didn't have a gaff hook or net so the boat was put on the beach and the fish was landed that way. I got out the first aid kit. Brian bandaged my fingers. After, we took the boat out into the evening sun and took this picture.

My first halibut.

Brother Brian with three 20 pound Red Snappers

A couple of days later, a plane took Brian home. July and August were very dry and hot. The creek almost dried up. Sockeye began collecting in the bay. When the tide was on the way up the salmon moved into the lagoon. When the tide dropped the fish swam back to the ocean. This continued day after day with more of these sockeye coming in each day. Apparently they would only go up when the water levels were high and the water temperature was lower.

One could see how the Indians once trapped fish with their rock walls in the lagoon.

Finally the rain began and the creek that had been reduced to a trickle filled with water again. A storm came up with wind and hard rain. Many sockeye were jumping in the bay. One could sense their urgency. When the tide was coming in I motored up to the lagoon. The creek was now running fast in reverse from all the new rain water. As the lagoon filled the salmon came in and started up the creek. I stayed there by myself watching this spectacle. The creek, now a raging torrent had more fish in it than water. Hour after hour the salmon came from the sea and headed, swimming and jumping into the creek to begin their journey to their spawning beds far above. I thought about what the Indian had said about walking across their backs. The air was filled with sea gulls and eagles. A large black bear showed up so I moved out.

The summer was over. I got help from a patrol boat to pack up the camp and was soon back at Bella Bella. From here I transferred to the Bonila Rock, another fisheries boat, and met an old friend, Leslie Kopas, who had also spent a summer as a Guardian. The Bonila took us to Bella Coola where I stayed for a few days with the Kopas family. I got a shave and a haircut.

The Union Steamship took Leslie and me to Vancouver where I started my fourth year at UBC.

SUMMER 1962

Finally, my university time was finished, A degree would be coming my way.

The end of the school year found me traveling by car to Kitimat, which was now my "home". During my first week back I spent a couple of days out at the Hotsprings renewing acquaintances. Here my old boss, Ray Skoglund asked if I wanted a summer job. This I accepted. Ray threw in a motel unit as well so I would be able to stay right at the Hotsprings.

In May the whole family, Mom and Dad and Brother Brian and I, motored down to Vancouver to attend the UBC graduation ceremonies. While down south we all drove down to Seattle to visit with relatives and spend some time at the Seattle's World Fair of 1962. I had already been down for a week during the last part of the school year. The NCAAU gymnastics championships were on and some of our BC gymnasts were competing. I got myself a week's pass to the Fair at that time.

While attending the fair a news broadcast came through that a huge slide had wiped out Lakelse

Hotsprings. I phoned back and found that was not true. There had been a slide. A mountainside had come down and had taken out the Provincial Park on the lake. When we arrived back we found out that the Hotsprings received no damage at all.

A cousin, Dick Hedstrom had been in the middle of the slide. The ground was about a square mile in area and nearly level and without any warning at all, started moving towards the lake. Trees remained standing. Large cracks appeared and geysers blew out of the road. These geysers were basically blue mud. Dick frantically ran down a road. He thought this was to safety. Ahead of him appeared a man running towards him who had the same idea. They both got out alive.

A week later in the early morning I was having coffee talking to a guest who was on his way out to the town of Terrace. This salesman left in his car. While we were still sipping on our coffees, our "guest" came back in a big hurry.

"A Slide! A Slide! The mountain has come down!"

"Yes, we had a slide a few weeks ago. Nothing to get excited about."

" "NO NO NO" The road is gone! This is a new slide!"

A few of the Hotsprings staff drove out to see what was wrong this time. A temporary road had been built above and around the first slide. The new road was missing. This second slide was worse than the first. The road ended in a hundred foot drop off. For a mile there was nothing but moving trees and mud that was all going out into the lake. A large tractor and earth mover were never seen again. No one was hurt. It was fortunate this happened early in the morning.

The second slide

Well, life must go on. One busy busy hot day the pools were completely full and there was a line up waiting to get in. I was sitting in the main chair on the main pool. Opposite me across the pool were doors to the change rooms. From the girls" side came this large Indian lady, about 400 pounds. She was wearing a "slip". She walked along the pool and went through the door way into the "hot pool area" There was a large window in the pool area wall. I watched her shuck off her slip. Oh Oh nothing on underneath. She jumped in the hot water.

Johnny, the new student life guard was doing his first morning on the hot pool.

He comes out, bright red, whistling and swinging his whistle on his finger… "Hey Monte, want to switch pools?" I told him, "No, not for a half an hour. You have to handle the problem."

On a more serious note, a week later, I was having breakfast early in the morning before the pools opened to the public. Johnny was out on the pool deck washing some windows. Three kids were in the pool. Two little ones were teaching their older big brother how to swim. The big one panicked, grabbed one of the little guys and was soon under water. The remaining boy screamed. I came out of the kitchen. Saw our lifeguard dive in. He headed to the bottom and managed to separate the two. I was running around the pool and got to a ladder just as Johnny arrived with the big unconscious boy. The little guy was okay. We hauled Big Boy out. His whole body was blue. I began mouth to mouth breathing with him. Big Boy came around puking water. As soon as he was able I drove him back to see his doctor in Terrace. The doctor just patted him on the head and told him not to do that again. The doctor received some nasty words from me.

As head guard at the resort many other jobs had to be done: cleaning, sweeping, cooking, cashiering, money counting, and painting signs.

This next story has nothing to do with any of that.

The Blue Man

One afternoon when I had some free time the manager asked me to show a guest to one of our tent cabins.

This was an old grizzled fisherman. He looked a bit like a grey version of Santa Claus. He had a Volkswagen camper van and was checking in to enjoy a bit of relaxation and swimming. I helped him pack a couple of suitcases into his tent cabin. He was quite proud of the contents of one piece of luggage and opened it up to show me what was inside. This suitcase was completely filled with bottles of liquer and liquor. He, we will call him Sam, told me that he had been "on the wagon" for five years and this was his time to celebrate. The management was informed. "As long as he does his drinking at that end of the camp, no problem."

This was on Monday night. At the end of the workday on Mondays an all night session was put in by one of the lifeguards. This time was my turn. Both our pools had to be drained, cleaned and refilled. This was done by noon the following day. The water was drained into an open ditch which ran down to Lakelse Lake. This was about a mile away. This ditch was quite deep, six feet or more and had a good layer of blue clay in the bottom which was quite slippery when wet. The water was always warm from the hotsprings.

I had started the process after everyone had gone to bed. After the water had gone down a foot, the sides were scrubbed clean with a bleach solution.

The process continued until the pools were empty. The drain was then shut and the water turned on allowing the water level to return to normal. The lights were on in the pool area and the lounge and restaurant. I had come out to the lounge for a smoke and a coffee. A radio was on loud to keep me awake. BANG BANG! What was that? BANG BANG! Someone was pounding on the front glass doors. On the outside with a large rock in his hand was a strange apparition. It was man-shaped. The colour though was blue. This creature was completely covered in blue clay. I realized this was Sam, our latest arrival. He wanted in. Under the blue clay was nothing! He was yelling something at me through the doors. I went upstairs to inform the manager. He phoned the cops. Our blue man did finally give up on the doors and made his way back down to his tent cabin.

The next morning some of our guests were telling of this strange being who had woken them up with the ungodly noise it was making. The noise and swearing were scaring the dogs. Someone saw him walking through the camp. At this time he had found a couple of cardboard boxes for shoes and was shuffling along. We guess the gravel had hurt his feet. His van was found on its side in our drainage ditch. Sam had backed into it in his foggy state and climbed out. He couldn't get out of the ditch. Too steep and too much blue mud. We could trace his route up to the pool complex. First his shirt, then his shoes and then his pants.

No one wanted to go and check him out so guess what? I had another job. This was to look after Sam. On reaching his tent cabin, I hollered. No answer. Is he in there? He must be, big blue footprints led to the door. I opened it and found Sam lying on his bed. He was naked and alive. I got him awake and told him that the cops were coming. They hadn't arrived yet from the night before. Sam got up, put on some cleaner clothes over the blue mud. He poured half a bottle of rum in a wash basin and cleaned up with that.

The cops arrived, one cop only. The cop asked me to go in and wake him up again because I knew him better. Sam yelled out. "I have rented this place. This is my home. You can't get me out without a warrant!"

I don't know the truth in this but the young constable went back to Kitimat to get one.

Later, a very apologetic Sam came in and asked to use the phone. "I have to get a wrecker to get my van out of the ditch." All we had was a radio phone and that was upstairs in the managers office. I went to make the call. Sam followed me. He started to walk in the door on the nice clean carpets.

"Sam, take your shoes off. They are all muddy."

He walked back to the outside door and took his shoes off and walked in to the phone desk. Oops, I had forgotten something. Sam, on his return to the phone left a trail of blue foot prints across the rug. Sam was still the blue man under his clothes. As he stood there waiting for me to make the call I could see that he was quite inebriated and smelled of booze. I think it was cream de menthe this time.

His lips were green. He mumbled thanks to me and weaved his way down the stairs and out.

I walked out on the outside pool deck to make sure that he was going back to his tent. "That was fast. I don't see him."

A half hour later, "Mr. Lifeguard, there is a dead man in the ditch!"

Oops, Sam had fallen in the blue ditch again. I went out to assist. Some kids were throwing rocks at him.

I hollered, "Cut that out!"

One kid said, "He's not dead. He is snoring.. Beside, his willy is poking out of his pants."

His willy was blue too. We got a blanket and covered Sam. I told the kids to skat. Later Sam did wake and made his way back to his tent.

Soon the wrecker came and pulled the Volkswagen out of the mud. Sam climbed in and was gone before the warrant arrived.

I will digress here a bit. In June an Australian comedian, arrived at the Kitimat High School to put on a performance. He was a friend of the Physical Education Teacher in the school. After the show, the Principal of the school, Roy Berry, talked with me for awhile. He asked me what my plans were after obtaining my degree. I told him that teaching would be nice but that another year was necessary for me to earn my teaching certificate.

"Keep us in mind when you are ready."

On August 22, a phone call was received from Mr. Berry. He asked me if I wanted to teach physical education and other subjects in September.

Before I could answer he said. "I know you are missing your last year but we are desperate! The school board will give you twenty-four hours to make up your mind." That evening I phoned back saying that I had accepted.

In between August 22nd and September 2nd I had gone down to Vancouver, got married to my wonderful girl, Coral and made my way back to Kitimat. This was another adventure. Maybe that story will be told later.

This all happened in my formative years. I do believe that the important parts of ones education are what happens in between the formal instruction periods. The in between parts are what makes a person who he is.

And so I would now start my career as a teacher.

MONTE ENGELSON

1962 photo by Mike Hoskins

Epilogue

Remember this picture? I was three when it was taken. Dad had just left for War II. Mom told me that I was now her Big Man. I figured I had to look grown up. So I did. This picture came back to me in a very strange way.

On Feb 6th 2012

I received an odd email from the UK. The gentleman, John Harold Herrick, who sent it asked a question.

"I have an interest in the family tree of the Engelsons' I have made a solid connection with your family, but it could be very sensitive and so before I go further I would like to know if you are still at this email address and if you are interested in communicating?"

Ah, a mystery!

I replied, "Yes!" The next day the answer came with two photographs. The first is below.

Above is writing fron the back of the picture, "Harold Engelson, Johnn's Dad, Brother.

This I recognized as one of my Dad in his RCAF uniform and his Brother, Bob. RCN.

With this pic was the pic of three year old me...
Both pictures were taken on the day Dad stepped on the train to Eastern Canada on his way to World War II in England. Uncle Bob, in the Navy uniform, had come up north to wish his brother a goodbye as there was a a good chance that his brother Harold, my Dad, would not be coming back. I can remember mom sending the pictures after she got them developed.
I will add another email from John.
February 7, 2012 Monte, Thanks for the positive response and I understand the comment about the waning interest in the family tree. For my part I have been putting it together for a while. Recently I have been trying to chase information for my Brother Terry. He recently died at the age of

76 after a great deal of fight on his part. He asked to continue finding information for him and I am 'pleased' to say I was able to find and give him the links he knew were there but not showing anywhere. I have been searching for details about my own past too. Now comes the difficult part. I am the result of a romantic liaison between my Mother Hilda and a Canadian airman in 1943. My Mother refused to speak about it directly to me except in short bursts, when obviously she tried to pluck up the courage. For my part I tried to cause her as little distress as possible and never pushed her for more information. Maybe I should have but it is of course too late now as she passed away in 1987. She gave me a picture of my Father, with a note in her writing, on the reverse. It reads 'Harold Engelson John's Dad —- Brother. (I attached the photo and reverse side note) . The story goes that she grieved following the loss of her husband in the Royal Navy 7 January 1943.

She continued to work as a head waitress throughout the War here in Lincoln. (Lincolnshire was known at the time as Bomber County) and at sometimes in Skegness, near Strubby Aerodrome. Where and how they met is not known. I was born in Carlisle on the borders of Scotland although we have no family connections there. However, Lincoln was bombed in the war and Carlisle was not, so maybe there was some reasoning along those lines. My mother told me that Harold was a very brave Man and that he was a Navigator, and was previously a 'Mounty" and loved the outdoors as I do. She said that he had seen me as a baby and they agreed to part because he had 'family'. Despite this I know she loved him until she died, as my sister-in-law confirms. They were extremely close. I suppose it was easier for my Mother to confide in another woman? My mother remarried to Phil Groves and had two more children by him. Until that time I was brought up as a Meanwell (my Mother's maiden name). On my part I was given the name 'Groves' when she married Phil Groves although he never truly accepted me, until I left education, when my birth certificate was needed for all legal matters when I reverted to the name on that document. 'John Harold Herrick'. No father is included. So I am a Herrick and there's an end to that part.

I have a second photo of Harold as a small boy which I also attach. My mother used to show this one when I was small and say with a twinkle in her eye, "Look at yourself John!"

Well, there it is. I may have opened pandora's box and you may wish to cease this communication and of course I would understand. For me I would like nothing more than to prove the situation one way or another

On another matter, I am in total admiration of your Mother who must have been a truly remarkable, gentle and strong character of which you must be proud.

It is strange, it has taken me a long time to compose this email and now I am in trepidation sending it, but here goes.

John.

A few pics from our past.

Dee, John, Monte, August 2015, Bella Coola

MONTE ENGELSON

John at two

Monte at six

Monte, Coral, Rodger, Cordelia

Jason, Dee, Jonathan, John

This "epilogue" is actually the beginning of another story or maybe many.

Please visit www.engelson.ca as this is where the stories begin.

And so concludes this book.
February, 4th 2016

www.ingramcontent.com/pod-product-compliance
Lightning Source LLC
LaVergne TN
LVHW021658060526
838200LV00050B/2409